The RV Upgrade Handbook Two

More Great Tricks You can do Yourself

Jay Bennett

The RV Upgrade Handbook Two
More Great Tricks You can do Yourself
by Jay Bennett

Published by:
Soquel Publishing Company
196 Nathan Ct
Soquel, CA 95073-2835
United States of America

Unattributed quotations are by Jay Bennett

ISBN, print ed.   978-0-9770578-1-8
ISBN, PDF ed.   978-0-9770578-3-2

First Printing 2013
Printed by: http://www.lulu.com
ID: 13660979

Printed in the United States of America

Library of Congress Cataloging-in-Publication Data

Library of Congress Control Number: 2013902586
Bennett, Jay.
The RV Upgrade Handbook Two: More Great Tricks You can do Yourself /Jay Bennett.

Table of Contents

Pictures and Diagrams

Introduction

Having now owned the same NuWa Hitchhiker 32 UKTG for the past nine years, it is time for some new information! Many modifications and enhancements have been made since my original book was published and I want to share them with you.

Every modification outlined in my first book is still in use today, after many miles and years of use. In fact I now have a small business and perform custom modifications for people who are not comfortable doing it themselves.

The tricks and techniques outlined herein have been applied to every sort of rig from high-end class A motor homes to small single room classic Airstreams. I am confident that you will find something in this book that you will want to try on your RV, no matter what size it is. This book is all new modifications on the same old rig!

Warning—Disclaimer

This book is full of opinion and practical applications. It includes many pictures and schematic diagrams. Many diagrams require some degree of technical ability to implement. The author shall have neither liability nor responsibility to any person or entity with respect to any loss or damage caused, or alleged to have been caused, directly or indirectly, by the information contained in this book.

The reader understands that while the author has tried and proven the information in this book, many of my ideas are creative, uncommon, and unconventional. Be warned that anything you do to your rig will be your own responsibility and will no doubt void your warranty. It is possible to damage parts and to injure yourself so please don't attempt anything unless you feel safe in doing so. Many RV shops can perform the work for you if you wish.

Some of my ideas and suggestions are not RIAA approved and would never pass muster for modern home building code inspection. Never-the-less they have been found to work safely and reliably when used as described. In fact you will find in many cases that a proper modification will actually improve the safety and reliability of your rig.

Chapter 1

Notes on my First Book

Tire Update

In my first book I said that tire under inflation is the single biggest contributor to tire failure. That remains true. However, I have found that running ten ply rated Load Range 'G' tires like the Goodyear G614 Unisteel at the full recommended pressure of 110 p.s.i. will cause blowouts as well.

Throughout my RV career I have had trouble with blowouts on my tows no matter how careful I have been with inflation and loading. I have spent thousands of dollars on various brands of RV tires and wheels. Let me share my experience with you so you can avoid this expense.

You must weigh your vehicle and make sure you are not exceeding the individual tire's weight rating. You will find that the load on each tire will vary up to ten percent from what you calculate from weighing the axle and dividing by two. This makes it imperative that you weigh each tire individually by maneuvering the rig onto the scale one side at a time to calculate the load on each tire.

My initial tires were four Goodyear G614's, rated at 3750 pounds each at 110 P.S.I. I have dual Dexter axles rated at 6000 pounds each. My weights were:

Right rear, 2970. Right front, 3150. Left rear, 2950. Left front, 2850. These weights are well within the limits of the G614's. The funny thing I noticed was that the tire with the *most weight on it had never blown out* (the right front) and over the years, *each of the other three had blown out.* This despite have used both a full set of new G614's, a full set of new Chinese Samson Load Range 'G' truck tires, and a full set of Michelin XPS RIB 245/75R16's during the period. I might add that the Michelins are the only tires that have never blown out.

Time to rethink this. Clearly overweight loading was not the factor causing the blowout. What was common to these blowouts? I had checked the tire inflation before each trip, in the morning before departure from my home near the coast in California. I made sure the tires were at 110 p.s.i., using a portable air compressor.

I parked the rig on plywood and jacked the tires off the ground during storage to avoid flat spots on the tires. I covered the wheels to avoid sun damage and to minimize ozone damage. Each tire looked like new. None of this had helped.

Each time I had a blowout I was on the freeway or interstate, traveling at 65 m.p.h. with light traffic. No stop and go. It was usually hotter than at my home. Where I live, the temperature is temperate, about 65 degrees year around and I am at sea level. Generally the blowout occurred when it was 90 degrees or more outside.

The tire would shed its tread; it was not a sidewall failure. What could be causing this?

I began to check tire pressures on the road. I would pull off the freeway and notice that the pressure has risen about 15 p.s.i. (to 135 p.s.i) due to the heat generated by the friction within the tire as it rolled down the road. I also noticed that when the outside temperature rose by 30 degrees, the tire pressure would rise another ten p.s.i. My tire pressure was almost 150 p.s.i. on a hot freeway day!

One failure occurred because the rubber valve stem had blown out of the wheel. Could over inflation be the culprit?

I noticed that Goodyear has a pressure de-rating chart for the G614, with the tire rated for only 3070 pounds (the Load Range 'E' maximum) when inflated to a reduced 80 p.s.i. Neither Samson nor Michelin had such a chart for their tires, but Michelin *did* have a chart for the XPS RIB that allowed for over inflation of up to 10 p.s.i. in Europe for increased speed ratings and with no reduction in weight rating.

The Michelin XPS RIB is a full steel Load Range 'E' tire, rated at only 3070 pounds at 80 p.s.i., just like my B.F. Goodrich Commercial TA LT265/75R16's that I use on the Dodge 2500 Diesel tow vehicle. Throughout this trailer blowout saga I had never blown out a Commercial T.A. at 80 p.s.i. despite their being continually overloaded by 10% on my truck drive axle. Maybe I was on to something.

I installed the Michelin XPS RIB's on the trailer and inflated them to only 80 p.s.i. even though I had 3150 pounds on one tire, a slight overload. Living life on the edge!

I took off on a summer trip from Santa Cruz, California (65 degrees out) to Dallas (105 degrees out.) As soon as I cleared Pacheco Pass into the central valley of California the temperature went up to 105°F and stayed there. I pulled off I5 and checked the XPS RIBs. The pressure had risen to 98 p.s.i. Ambient heat and road friction heat DID matter. The tires stood tall but still had full tread contact. They felt quite warm to the touch but not too hot to handle.

Four thousand road miles in three weeks. Some days traveling 600 miles. No daytime temperatures under 100. Long non-stop stretches in Texas with the air conditioner maxed out all day. Blasting over Loveland Pass on I70 at 10,000 feet. Lots of bugs on the 5er. Carried two spares. No blowouts.

So I don't really have any tire preferences between Michelin, Goodyear, and Goodrich, but I do believe that none of the above mentioned tires should ever be allowed to exceed 110 p.s.i. hot.

My new rule of thumb is to inflate any of them to 85 p.s.i. cold before your day on the road and to check them hot. Remember that the pressure may rise to dangerous levels if there is a significant increase in outside temperature or a 5000 foot elevation increase.

As I said in my first book, most trailers ship with tires that are barely adequate to carry the vehicle off the lot. Manufacturers generally use the cheapest tire available. They call them 'ST' for 'Special Trailer' and they are only speed rated to 55 m.p.h. While they may be adequate for very short day trips, they are inadequate for any great distance. Car and truck tires have an overload safety margin that allows operation at full rated load continuously.

Light truck tires are preferred for trailers with the only disadvantage being stiffer sidewalls, which may increase undercarriage stresses when the trailer is cornered sharply as when parking. In my repair business I *have never* seen any mechanical damage caused by the use of truck tires on trailers. I *have* seen bent spring hangers from trailers trying to back over curbs and berms. I *have* seen broken springs from large potholes. I *have* seen bent rear axles from backing a dual or triple axle trailer up a steep incline. Stiff sidewalls would not have mattered in these cases.

So check those pressures. Avoid over inflation as well as under inflation.

Other Notes

My first book was geared toward the use of a single 30 amp park power source. In this book I will show you many tricks to fully utilize available park power sources to maximize the usage of available power.

Power converters have also evolved since the first book as has the practice of using of multiple small generators instead of a single large one.

I am still not a real solar panel fan and the reasoning remains unchanged: they are very expensive for what they deliver.

Lighting has evolved to the use of LED's for illumination. They only use 5% as much electricity as incandescent bulbs, but are ten times as expensive and offer less light. They can however make a huge difference in the amount of electricity you need to generate. They also measurably reduce the interior heat load in the summertime.

I still use the same Dodge Ram towing vehicle. I have done many more modifications to this truck to make it reliably tow a large fifth wheel. Nearly every modification outlined in my first book remains in service today, many miles down the road.

The major components that have been replaced include the injection pump and the transmission/torque converter.

The injection pump failed abruptly as I was parking my rig at home. Perfect timing. It was the victim of a series of poor replacement stock lift pumps. The new Blue Chip Diesel injection pump is fueled by a Glacier 'gerotor' (Raptor) lift pump kit.

The transmission served admirably for 100,000 miles without modification other than a high pressure valve body with shift kit and a Suncoast single plate torque converter. Then it became erratic on 1-2 shifts. The second gear clutches were heat damaged as was the rear band due to maladjustment. The transmission was rebuilt locally using DTT long life components. Torque converters had evolved considerably and the single plate Suncoast was replaced with a triple plate Goerend unit.

My main vocation and avocation remains RV maintenance.

Chapter 2

Water and Gas Tricks

Shower Booth

We do a lot of dry camping. One of the most often commented modifications I have made is the outside shower booth. Many people have an outside shower fixture but how many have an installed portable shower booth to go with it? My OEM exterior shower fixture was installed near the front door, which is great for washing dirty feet but impractical for showers. After all who wants a big water puddle at your doorstep?

The shower booth modification is inexpensive to build assuming you have already installed the outside shower fixture in an appropriate location away from your entry door, preferably on the road side of your rig. If not, I use Phoenix #377 outside shower assemblies when I install them.

The key element of the booth is the curtain bar. It is made from an eight foot length of 3/4 inch I.D. PEX tubing which is readily available at Home Depot. You will also need 2 each 22" lengths of ½ inch copper tubing (bend it as straight as possible!), which are glued into each end of the PEX with epoxy or household goop. The copper tubing provides the extra rigidity to support the shower curtain without droop while still allowing the PEX to be bent into a semi-circle for insertion into the base mounts.

The base mounts are screwed onto the side of the rig 36 inches apart and 80 inches above the ground, centered on your outside shower fixture, using stainless steel hardware. The base mounts are Suncor stainless steel stanchion base rail mounts (sailboat hardware) part number 755983 or equivalent 7/8 inch i.d. 90 degree. The base mount side holes come tapped for ¼ x 28tpi screws. Hex head cap screws (common 1 ½ inch hex head bolts ¼ x 28) are used to secure the PEX into the base (hand tighten only!) while capturing the first shower curtain ring.

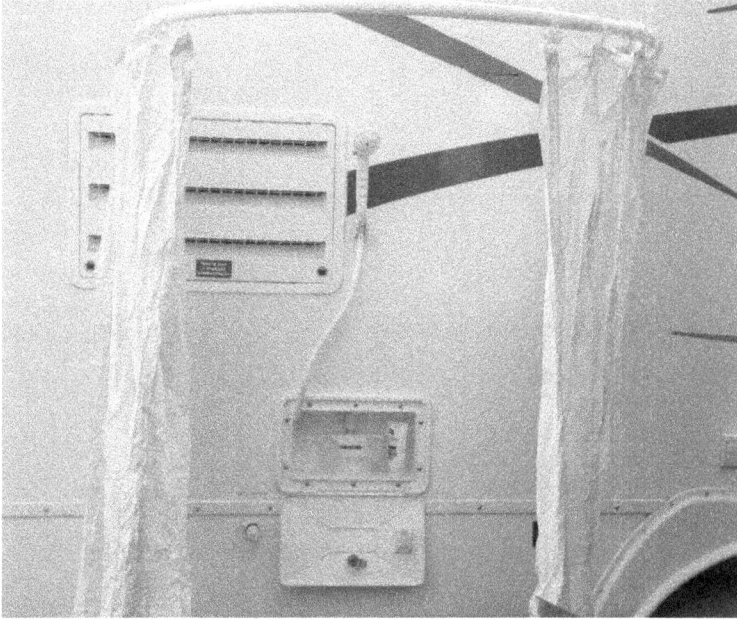

The cheap plastic shower curtains are fitted with small brass eyelets around the bottom (available at any sewing/notions retailer,) which allow small 1/8 bungee cords to be secured to tent stakes. These bungees keep the curtain from blowing around in windy weather.

This system is tried and true. To spiff it up you may want a folding wooden shower step, which can also be used to store the curtains. The PEX bar is stored in the basement in its curved state. I was lucky enough to have some space on the basement ceiling where I mounted some loops of plumbers tape. The ends of the PEX semicircular loop are inserted into the plumbers tape loops, which secure it overhead and out of the way.

Outside Hose Bib

Every rig is equipped with a low point drain in the water system to allow the water system to be winterized. I was lucky because these drains were located in a place that easily allowed them to serve double duty as hose bib valves.

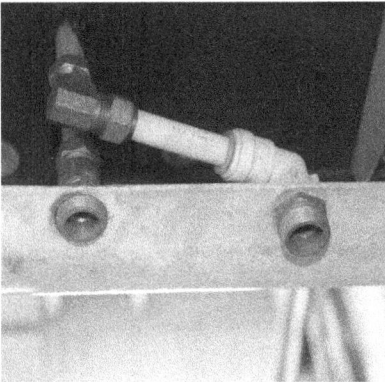

I simply used PEX compression fittings to adapt the PEX tubing drain pipes to a brass hose fitting, running it through the fairing sheet metal for added rigidity. This allows use of an exterior sink, ability to fill buckets with water, hot or cold, watering plants, washing bugs off with a garden hose, or even the use of an outside washing machine! All while still dry camping. Also, no need to disconnect your rig from the city water to use the hose when in a park with water hookups.

Gas Manifold Valve

Everyone nowadays seems to have a need for propane outside, whether for barbeques, stoves, or heaters. It's a lot less expensive to use your on-board propane for these appliances, which you can refill at bulk rate prices, than to buy small containers of propane for each appliance. Why haul these extra containers around? Why run out of propane for a particular appliance when you have a full supply onboard your RV available?

Nearly all propane appliances can be converted using commonly available pipe fittings, to use propane supplied via hose. The propane supplied by your regulated RV propane system is already at the ideal pressure for most appliances. Therefore additional regulators are not used, nor necessary. Any appliance that uses a propane tank with an attached regulator is an ideal candidate for a hose connection. Since the pressure used is less than 5 P.S.I., the likelihood of fire or explosion due to leaks is minimal. You must however be careful no to allow leakage to occur inside your RV in a contained space.

Use only hose that is made for explosive gases. Such hose can be obtained from a welding supply house by the foot. I use red 3/16 inch acetylene hose for all applications, even large multi-burner camping stovetops.

I have modified a Weber "Q" grill and a tabletop radiant heater to attach to my manifold. See pictures. Both use ¼ inch pipe fittings with hose barbs for connection to the gas hose and a hose barb on a 3/8 flare fitting for connection to the manifold. No clamps are used.

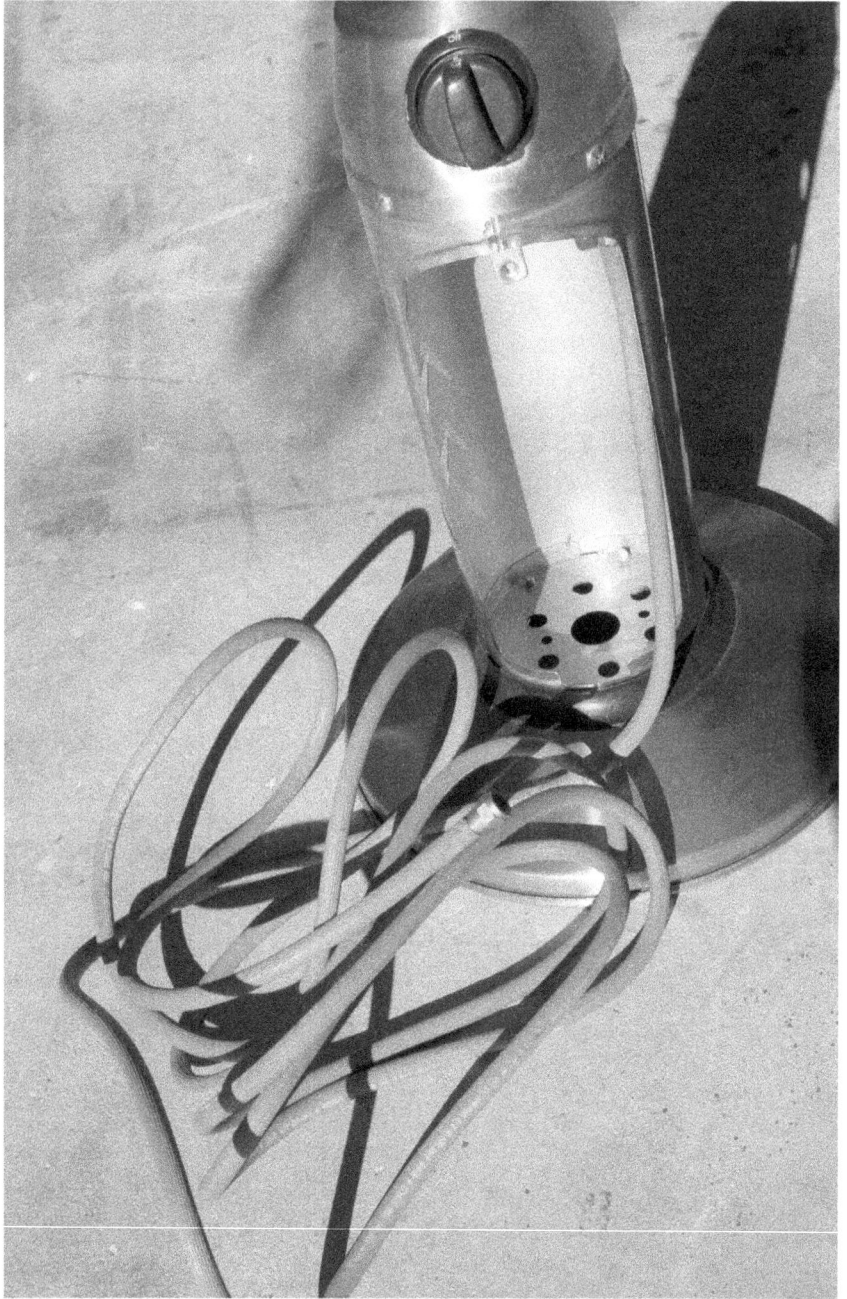

The valve is a common 3/8 gas valve; the plumbing is 3/8 pipe connected to the ½ inch propane piping system. The manifold consists of 3/8 flare fittings which are capped when not used. The "Q" grill sits atop a sliding metal frame.

The Sliding Frame

The frame that holds the "Q" grill is made of 1" angle iron welded atop a ¼ inch thick steel plate. The plate has a single ¾ inch hole, which is mated to another ¼ inch steel plate below through a single large pivot bolt. The lower plate is attached to vertically mounted heavy-duty drawer slides, which are lag bolted to the basement floor using angle iron and ¾ inch plywood as a base.

The frame allows the whole grill/frame assembly to slide outside the basement when in use; after sliding out, the top frame/plate assembly pivots in the horizontal plane around the single ¾ inch pivot bolt 90 degrees so that the grill faces the cook. The lower plate and upper plate are drilled through at certain pivot angles e.g. at 45° and 90° where a through bolt is inserted to stabilize the plate at defined working angle. Folding 1" strap braces are fitted for stability.

Incidentally, the sliding/pivoting frame serves many appliances besides the "Q" grill, including a two burner camp stove and a Vizio 32" HDTV. The sliding/pivoting frame allows quick setup and secure locked storage for any appliance on the sliding frame. It proves very handy for quickly grilling burgers on the road. In the campground it allows for the outside HDTV to be locked away quickly inside the basement for secure storage.

Grey Water Plus

My particular rig has two grey water tanks. The galley tank is rated at 30 gallons and the shower/lavatory/washing machine tank is 40 gallons. I find that I fill up the galley tank faster than the lavatory tank. All holding tanks share a common drain pipe and manifold, with each tank emptying into the common manifold through individual drain valves.

Some dry camping areas will allow draining grey water onto the ground if it contains no food waste, hence the use of two separated tanks. This separation makes it possible to drain only lavatory/shower/washing machine water onto the ground while retaining food waste water for later disposal along with the black waste water. Other dry camping areas will allow no grey water to be drained onto the ground whatsoever. With this restriction, it is convenient to make both grey water tanks a common reservoir, allowing the total capacity of both banks to accumulate grey water from both the galley and the lavatory systems.

To make this possible, I added a master drain valve near the drain outlet. With this valve closed and both grey tank valves open, the grey tanks can equalize between themselves, making the total capacity the sum of both tanks plus the manifold. It does not matter if one tank is mounted higher than the other; the lower tank merely fills first followed by the higher tank. This entire filling sequence can be monitored using the existing tank level monitors. See below.

It is important to keep the grey tanks clean, especially if you are filling both tanks with galley waste. Galley waste usually contains food particles and grease, which will eventually deposit on the tank walls and cause faulty tank monitor readings. The only way to keep these tanks clean is by generous flushing and the use of formaldehyde based tank deodorants.

I advise mounting power tank flush rinsers such as the Camco 40123. The rinser flush head is mounted in the tank so that the head forces water directly at the monitor sensors. Careful measuring is needed to mount the flush head at the correct location in the tank, ideally at a 45 degree angle toward the sensors. Extra holes may be drilled into the flush head to get the desired water spray direction.

All tanks should have this type of power rinser if you plan to get accurate readings from your tank level monitoring system. They ALL get cruddy eventually so the sooner you install them, the better. Drilling extra holes and adding additional sensors is only a temporary fix; Even capacitive electronic pickup systems like the SeeLevel system require a clean tank wall (no crud) at the sensor location if you expect accurate readings.

Water Pump Tap

How often do you need to refill your water tank while dry camping?

We were at Woodward Campground in the undeveloped area. We had a beautiful spot with our own private beach and set up under a shade tree. Life could not be better! We decided to have a mini birthday party for our son and invited friends and relatives.

Since we had been set up for six days we were running low on water. We decided to take a bladder in the pickup bed to get ourselves a forty gallon refill. After filling and returning we backed up the truck next to the rig and could not find a way to get the water from the water bladder into the water tank! The truck bed was lower than the water fill, even though the RV tank itself was lower than the bladder.

I had a way to suck water into the rig water pump using a wye valve and exterior auxiliary water fill which I described in my first book, but the pump was not able to suck the water through all that hose and uphill through the fill, which was mounted 2 feet higher than the pump. Besides, if I needed groceries, I would have to disconnect the water bladder and take it along to the store. All this was very unsatisfactory.

After much consternation, my wife suggested that I park the truck on an adjoining hill and run 150 feet of hose to the rig. With lots of siphoning it finally worked. But it was way annoying.

Time to rethink the water pump thing. I had installed the auxiliary water inlet to allow filled water bladders on the roof of the rig to pump directly into the RV water system. This had worked for me for years but always required that I estimate my total water usage when I arrived to dry camp so that I could fill the requisite number of bladders on the roof before setting up camp. And I had always had trouble priming the pump because of the loop of hose drooping onto the ground and up to the auxiliary inlet fitting. The pump was trying to lift the water two feet above itself to prime and the line always had air in it. I needed to move the pump inlet down to a point about level with the pump on the floor of the RV.

I removed the auxiliary inlet fitting and mounted a JR products 95185 drain port at the location of the old auxiliary inlet. See below.

I had to reduce the ¾ inch port hose barb to ½ inch hose barb inside using a reducing elbow to adapt to ½ inch hose. I teed off the water pump ½ inch output hose and inserted a small gate valve in the line to the drain port.

The drain port with its male hose threads had morphed into a water pump outlet pressure port, and it was located immediately adjacent to the water tank fill door. I mounted a small gate valve in the new outlet line near the pump inlet wye valve (see book 1) under the kitchen sink on the floor for easy access.

Next I relocated the old auxiliary inlet fitting (a JR products 160-85-A-16-A city water flange with the check valve removed) down at floor level (see above.) This became the new pump inlet port. I reused the screen faucet washer to keep out any debris.

It works great! I connect a small piece of hose from the pump outlet port to the water fill and connect a hose from the water bladder in the pickup bed to the water inlet port. Turn the pump inlet wye valve to auxiliary, open the outlet gate valve, and turn on the pump. Since the pump and the water bladder are at nearly the same level there is no problem with priming the pump and the whole bladder is pumped dry into the rig water tank in short order.

This set up gives you lots of flexibility for the use of your water pump when dry camping such as sharing your water with your friend in the pop-up tent trailer. You always have the ability to bring more potable water to your site and to refill your tank.

Shower Anti Siphon Valves

Somewhere during my long lifetime someone got smarter than all of us and ordained that all shower faucet assemblies should have vacuum breakers to keep us from poisoning our RV water supply. This problem might allegedly occur if we somehow dipped our shower hose into the toilet and shut off the RV water supply, creating a vacuum in the RV water system. I categorize vacuum breakers in the same waste basket as water restrictors and GFI receptacles i.e. items that cause RVs far more trouble than their safety value is worth.

In all of my RV experience I have never seen anyone suck any water *into* a shower hose. What I *have* seen is a lot of frustrated campers trying to wipe up the constant water leak from the top of the shower faucet or paying huge sums to have the wood rot repaired from a leaky shower fixture.

Two weeks ago a lady called me because she had no water service in her rig. She and her husband were full timers. She had to turn off the water supply because shower water was blowing all over her bathroom. When I arrived I found that the Utopia shower faucet had been taken apart and the plastic valve stems were broken in half. I asked her what had happened and she said that she had taken the faucet apart to fix the constant leak out of the top of the faucet. I told her that it may not be possible to repair the faucet and its replacement involved removing the shower surround from her twenty year old coach to access the plumbing, an expensive proposition. Fortunately the valve seats were undamaged and the Utopia valve stem parts were still available. Two days and $200 later she was up and running....

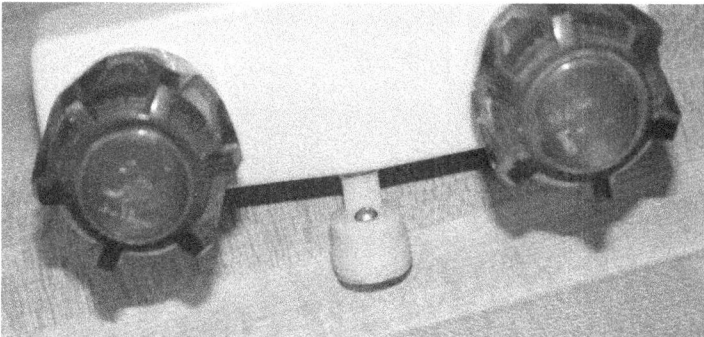

Now you could just replace the vacuum breaker with a riser spud such as the Phoenix 9-44-13 and be done with it. But it's much quicker to just put a ¼ inch #8 screw in the hole on the breaker underside and save the money. Use a dab of silicone seal before tightening. The breaker is 1/8 pipe threads and can just be unscrewed from the top of the faucet using pliers. See above. Just beware that blocking that hole may get you in trouble with the sanitation police!

Holding Tank Heat

For many of us the idea of heating the holding tank area is pretty foreign. After all who lives in RV's in the winter-time anyway? Most lower end rigs are not weather proofed and if yours fits into this category you will face considerable work to winterize your rig.

Our first trailer was a used 14 foot Prowler tail dragger. We bought it on the cheap in the fall and decided to take it to Sun River, Oregon, to join the family for a Christmas ski vacation at Mt. Bachelor. Being complete novices to RVing was no hindrance and we set off up I5 from our California home to the Oregon high desert. As we went further North on US97, the slush turned to hard packed snow and we didn't even think about the holding tank until we were set up next to the family cabin at Sun River.

As the temperature fell into the low 20's it occurred to us that our holding tank might freeze. Panic! What to do? The water tank was inside so no problem as long as we had propane to keep the primitive Suburban furnace running. We drove to Goodwill and bought an old queen sized electric blanket. I stapled it around the rear perimeter, surrounding the holding tank and plugged it in to stolen power from the cabin. The blanket kept it ten degrees warmer than outside and luckily we set off for home before the really cold weather arrived.

Our current NuWa rig is weather-proofed, meaning it has treated cardboard with a laminated layer of insulated foil screwed onto the frame rails the complete length underneath. These cardboard panels completely enclose the under floor area and provide semi-sealed ten inch deep space full length which is packed with three holding tanks, water tank, plumbing, tank drain manifolds, wire runs, and central heat ducting, etc. NuWa, headquartered in Kansas, gave considerable forethought to the problems of freezing weather. The heat ducting is routed through the space to allow the ducts to radiate waste heat into the holding tank space. While there are no direct heat registers in the space, the heated ducting is sufficient to provide ten to fifteen degrees of ambient heat rise for the holding tanks. Since there is also heat loss from the living space through the floor, the ambient can rise even further. This combination allows the coach to be used in the winter as long as the outside temperature is above 10°F and the propane furnace is keeping the interior at 65°F or higher.

The propane furnace is very inefficient and uses LOTS of propane under these conditions, nearly seven gallons in two days. So we all try to plug into the park's electricity to supplement and/or replace the propane furnace with electric heat. Very inefficient but possibly less expensive to the RVer. The down side to electric heat is a reduction of heating capacity in the holding tank space.

However, the real reason for building a *supplemental* electric holding tank heater is not to make up for reduced use of the propane furnace, it is to insure against freezing the tanks and tank drain manifolds while the rig is in unattended storage in more moderate climates.

My buddy in California goes through a complete winterizing schedule with his trailer each year even though he parks his rig next to his house, has a single 100 watt solar panel, and the outside temperature rarely goes below 32°F. When it does freeze out, it is for a brief period at night or early morning. The next day, temperatures rise back into the 40s. He would like to use his rig for some winter camping but has to flush and refill everything each time he does so. His trailer is winterized with insulated holding tank space panels. He is an ideal candidate for a holding tank space heater.

The heating element is a 2 ohm 225 watt edge wound resistor such as the Ohmite 270 series (Digikey Part L225J2RO-ND also use mounting bracket 18E-100-ND). These resistors are about $20 each and supply about 90 watts of heat per resistor, each drawing about 7 amps from the battery. The relay is a common black 30 amp automotive relay from O'Rielly. One relay can control up to four resistors. The relay is controlled by an 'on-auto' switch from inside the rig and also by a thermostat in the holding tank space. The thermostat is a common millivolt heater thermostat, commonly found on a household wall heater (about $25.) The thermostat has to be modified so that it will open and close in the range of 20° to 60° instead of 50° to 90° as supplied.

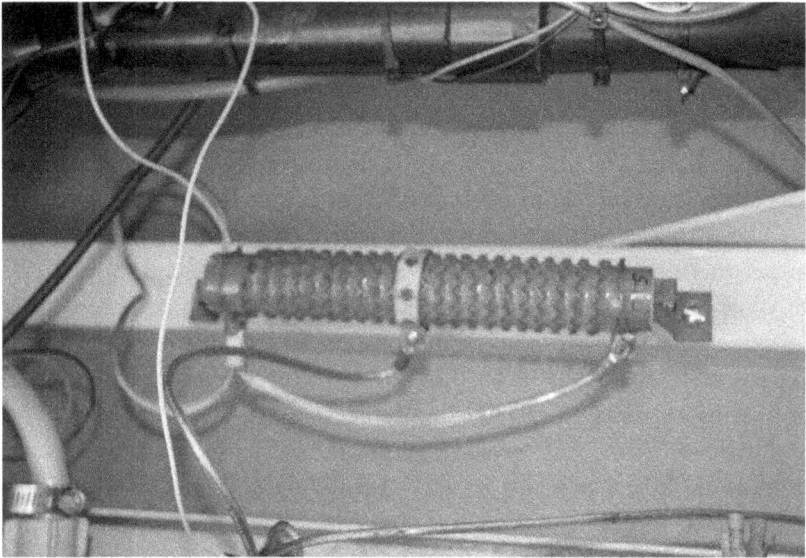

This is done by removing the plastic covers and removing the heat sensing coil assembly from the thermostat. Using needle nose pliers, shift the position of the adjusting arm on the sensing coil shaft. Only a slight shift of about 20 angular degrees is necessary. Reassemble and test by placing the unit inside your refrigerator. Note the point where the thermostat audibly clicks and mark it at 40°F. Use a meat thermometer if you are not sure of the temperature inside your refer. You may need to repeat the procedure a couple of times until you get the thermostat to click at 40° in the center of its range of adjustment. When you are satisfied, rescale the thermostat with a marking pen.

Wire it up as shown in the schematic diagram below. I duct taped the thermostat so that it is face down on the inside of the cardboard holding tank space cover, after cutting a small slit in the cardboard to allow adjustment of the thermostat set point without removing the cover. The thermostat should be located well away from the heating resistor(s), preferably under a holding tank, and at a low point in the holding tank area. Just tape over the slit from underneath when finished adjusting. I set it at 35°F.

The heater uses the coach battery for power, therefore you must have your rig plugged in or have sufficient solar capacity to make up for the heater drain. I find that one 90 watt resistor is adequate to cause a 9° temperature rise in the holding tank space, with no other heating supplied and the rig heat turned off. This is perfect for rig storage in my temperate Northern California climate where I never see temperatures below the mid 20's. I am confident that a single resistor would be adequate for most locations in the Southern Continental U.S. and is great insurance for those brief winter freezes in the South and desert regions.

Holding Tank Heater Circuit

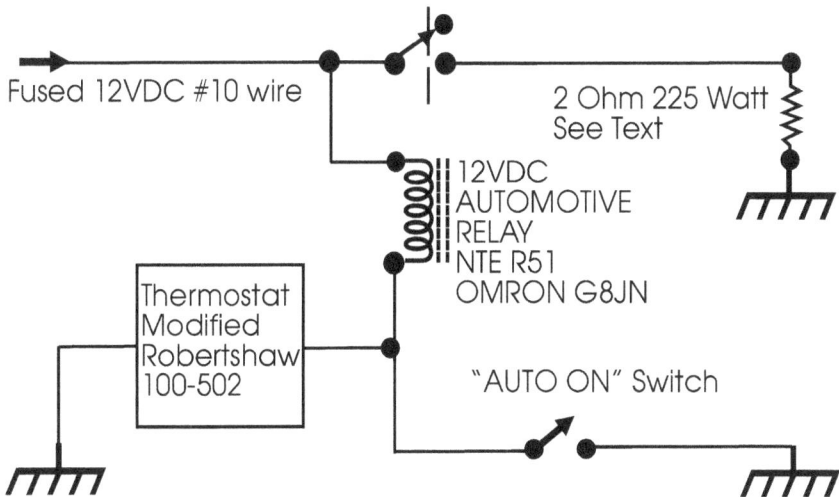

Fused 12VDC #10 wire

2 Ohm 225 Watt
See Text

12VDC
AUTOMOTIVE
RELAY
NTE R51
OMRON G8JN

Thermostat
Modified
Robertshaw
100-502

"AUTO ON" Switch

Install an inexpensive remote reading digital thermometer inside your rig so you can monitor the holding tank space temperature. Some thermometers even have an audible alarm when they detect freezing temperatures.

Manually turning on the holding tank space heater the afternoon before a night-time big freeze will reserve you extra time at below freezing temperatures that night.

Gas System Purging

When we store our rigs we generally turn off the propane supply at the tanks. The propane system on most rigs seeps a small amount of propane all the time. The leakage is normal, very low, and doesn't present a safety hazard. Never-the-less, after the propane has been shut off for an extended period (or we have run out of propane), it will become necessary to purge the air from the propane lines to restore normal operation.

First, turn on the propane supply. Next, turn on the burners on your propane stovetop. At first you will get nothing but air. Keep constantly attempting to light the burners until they ignite. This process may take 15 to 30 seconds depending on the length of pipe from your propane tanks to the stove. If you smell gas, stop! The burners should have lighted by now.

Next, turn on the propane appliance that is farthest away from the supply tank. It may take two or three attempts to start it. You are now finished purging.

Don't attempt to start (or restart) your gas refrigerator until you have already purged the system with higher demand appliances. The gas refrigerator uses so little propane that you will become frustrated with multiple futile restart attempts. You may also lock out the refrigerator, requiring a power down of the refer control board to reset it.

I know this tip might be old news for many of you, but I see this problem time and again so it is worth remembering.

Chapter 3

Multiple Charge Sources

People seem to get the term converter and inverter mixed up all the time. Converters are devices similar to sophisticated battery chargers that convert household power into a form that can be used to supply the devices that work on 12 volt style car battery power. The converter's main job in an RV is to change household or park supplied AC power into direct current that can charge the batteries in the RV. The batteries then supply the power to run 12 volt devices.

An inverter does the exact reverse. It converts RV battery power into household current that can be used by common household appliances. Inverters will be discussed later; they are an enhancement that not all RV's are equipped with. However, every RV has some form of converter supplied when it is delivered.

The telephone company has been doing this battery charging thing for years. The whole telephone system runs on 48 volts DC and could run on 4 car batteries connected together in a string, if the car batteries were big enough. The phone company takes household power similar to your own and uses a whole group of converters to charge its behemoth battery string. The telephone equipment that supplies dial tone, ISP service, and long distance/broadband connections all run on this battery power. That is why the phone and internet service keeps running during a general power failure. It's that huge string of batteries that keeps everything alive. The phone company likes redundancy; that's why it uses a *group* of converters. If one fails, the others have enough reserve capacity to make up the lost charging power.

When the power fails at the telephone company, huge generators come to life automatically and re-supply the converters with in-house generated power. The converters and their batteries don't care who gives them household power, as long as it come from somewhere and arrives before the batteries lose their charge.

So our trick in RVing is just the same: to re-supply our batteries before they discharge. Deep cycle RV batteries do not enjoy being completely discharged. If we discharge batteries to less than half full repeatedly we will reduce their service life. So we strive to have enough batteries to supply our needs until we can recharge them, or we keep a converter operating all the time to prevent them from discharging at all.

There is no law that says that we cannot use more than one charging source on a battery. Most RVs have more than one way to recharge their batteries. As a minimum a trailer will have a converter as well as a wire from the towing vehicle (called the charge line) and these are both connected simultaneously. Even the simplest converter stops charging at some set point and cannot be hurt by another converter, alternator, or solar charge controller trying to charge in parallel. The batteries don't even have to be connected at all for a converter to convert. And each charging device has a built-in 'trap door' that allows current to flow only one way: OUT.

If there is any trickery at all involved with multiple charging sources, it is figuring out how to prioritize them so we can control which one comes on first, second, and so on.

Lets look at a very basic setup: An unregulated (no charge controller) solar panel, a Magnetek 7345 series converter, and a 12 volt trailer battery. This setup is common on many rigs.

Neither one of these charging sources has a method for the user to adjust the charging voltage. Let's look at each source individually first, and finally we will look at the combined behavior.

The 7345 is a switching converter which means it has very high efficiency, over 85%. This means that 85 or more percent of the household current is consumes is converted into battery power. This is considered a very high and a very 'green' conversion efficiency. The 7345 produces an output voltage of 13.7 volts and is not adjustable.

Lead-acid (and AGM) batteries reach full charge at 13.2 volts. Therefore the 7345 will always be trying to overcharge the battery and it has 45 amps worth of push to do it. This practice of overcharging is commonplace with lead-acid technology chargers; a car alternator tries to charge at 14 volts if it can, all the time. The down side to continuous forced overcharging is water loss. (Remember, 'Maintenance Free' is an oxymoron.) The battery will have to be checked and refilled with distilled water every six months. You will notice boil over liquid on top of the battery and possibly corrosion of the battery box and terminals. However, as long as the water level is maintained, the battery is fine. Incidentally, exposed plates inside the battery mean immediate battery replacement.

Now as soon as you turn on your coach lighting, the battery voltage will drop off to a nominal 12.7 volts. If the 7345 is running the battery voltage will not drop off at all until your current demand exceeds the 45 amp capacity of the 7345, at which time the battery voltage will drop as the battery supplies the additional current demand. When the load ceases, the 7345 will refill the battery and happily begin to overcharge again.

So how much current can we safely continually push into a lead-acid or AGM battery without damage? It depends on the size. All batteries self discharge over time. Those of us that live in freezing climates know that a discharged battery will freeze no matter its age. So it is desirable to trickle charge these batteries if we can do so without boiling off all the water. As you can see, 45 amps at 13.7 volts is too much. I have determined experimentally that ½ amp (500 milliamps or ma) of current will not cause significant water loss on a group 24 or group 27 car battery, the size typically used in an RV.

As batteries age, their internal resistance rises due to their plates becoming coated with a non-conductive layer of sulfur. This process is called sulfation. As this process advances the battery takes more and more energy to recharge, mainly due to the charger having to overcome the extra resistance created by the layer of sulfur. This process also results in a battery which cannot deliver high current when a load such as a starter or inverter demands it. Inevitably the battery will need replacement.

But we are discussing trickle chargers. As the battery ages it will take a higher voltage to overcome the increased internal resistance and achieve our target of 500 ma of trickle current. A small unregulated solar panel achieves this nicely for two reasons. First, the current that a solar panel produces is directly related to the size of the panel. A fifteen inch square panel will produce no more than 1 amp in direct sunlight and more like 500 ma in average light. In addition, a nominal 12 volt solar panel will deliver up to 22 volts into an open circuit. Of course, a connected battery is not an open circuit but as it ages, the solar panel's voltage can rise to overcome the aging process and continue to deliver trickle charge into an older battery. Thus a *properly sized* unregulated panel is a perfect trickle charger.

As you may have guessed, as we add more or larger batteries, we need to increase the size of the panel to keep this nice balance of charging current. A string of six group 27 or golf cart batteries will need a 100 watt 2 by 4 foot panel. A pair of 4d's or 8d's will also require a 100 watt panel, just for charge maintenance.

Also, as we increase the size of the solar panel we start to flirt with the danger of exposing our 12 volt devices (loads) to excessive and damaging voltage from an unregulated panel. This damage could occur if the batteries were disconnected from the panel while the panel was still connected to the loads. That is why properly installed solar panels are always connected directly to the battery terminals. That way if the batteries are removed, the panel is disconnected as part of the removal process.

As we increase the size of the battery string, increasing our need for trickle charge current from 500 ma to 3 amps, it becomes less important for the open circuit voltage to rise to 22 volts from an unregulated panel. In fact, it only takes about 14.5 volts to 'boost charge' a large battery string and delay sulfation. Therefore it is good practice to add a regulator to the larger panel and adjust it to a 14.5 volt maximum output voltage, to protect our 12 volt device loads. However, regulators use energy from the solar panel to do their job, so we don't use them on small panels since they may consume a significant fraction of the panel's capacity just to operate.

Of course if the single solar panel grew into a large solar array, regulation becomes a requirement. Such large arrays essentially turn into the equivalent of the 7345 we discussed earlier and lose the ability to be trickle chargers.

Solar panels are not inherently prevented from consuming energy from your batteries in the absence of sunlight. There is no 'trap door.' You must install a 'trap door' yourself on unregulated panels; A 100 or 1000 piv 1 amp silicon diode (about 5 cents at Radio Shack) will serve nicely for a small panel. Make sure the end with the band on it faces toward the battery. Panel arrays with regulators usually have some sort of built in trap door.

In our simple battery/7345/15 inch solar panel system it is perfectly fine to have all three wired together all the time. We just must use a trap door diode on the solar panel. See below.

Battery Disconnect if equipped
Point 'A'.   100 PIV 1A diode

```
Parallax      Parallax          +              15 Watt
Power    →    Power    ⊥ 12 Volt               Solar
7345    To    Fuse     ⊤ Battery               Panel
        Load  Panel  ▲
        Devices     Vehicle
                    Charge
                    Line
```

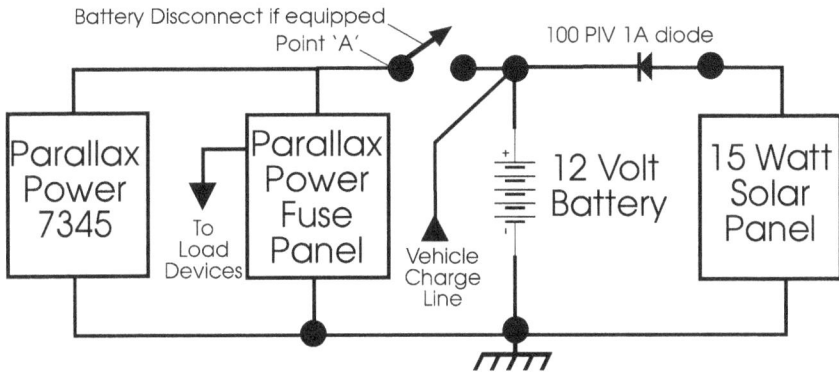

When household current is connected, the 7345 happily overcharges our battery and supplies most of our 12 volt needs. When we are unplugged, the battery supplies our needs, with a small insignificant amount of help from the solar panel. When we are plugged into our towing vehicle (with the engine running) the vehicle alternator supplies current to the battery through a charging line, usually supplying as much current as the 7345.

When we are stored, and not plugged in, the solar panel trickle charges the battery. So the whole system is fairly maintenance free. We still need to check the battery water level every six months.

There are some caveats. You may have forgotten to shut down your refrigerator or unplug/defuse your propane or CO detector. These devices use 12 volt power from your battery and the 15 watt solar panel will not supply enough power to run these devices.

Some people use a battery disconnect to isolate the battery from the load fuse panel during storage. Other just remove the fuses that power these devices. In any case you will need to do a 'sneak current' analysis to make sure you have shut down anything that consumes 12 volt power during storage, or risk a dead battery.

To test for sneak currents, you must first isolate the wire that runs from the battery to 12 volt load fuse panel. See Point 'A' in the diagram above. Then remove this wire from the battery. Make sure that the rig is disconnected from household or park power. Make sure the rig is unplugged from the towing vehicle. Connect an ammeter like a Fluke 73 (0-10 amp range) between the battery post and the load wire to the fuse panel. Of course, if you have a battery disconnect, you can just insert the ammeter across the opened disconnect. The meter should read zero. If it reads more than zero you will need to find the device in your coach that is consuming power and shut it down.

Converters in Parallel

Converters come in various capacities and configurations. The larger they are the more charging current they can provide and the more current they can consume from the household/generator supply. From my first book you will remember that a converter like a 7345 Parallax draws nearly 7.3 amps from the AC source, slightly more than a Honda 1000 generator can deliver.

Now we see that it is perfectly safe and normal to use multiple methods and different devices to recharge our battery string; the main consideration being our ability to prioritize which charging device takes over first, second, and so on. And these devices can be connected simultaneously to the battery string as long as we are sure that a 'trap door' is in place to prevent a charging device from becoming an unwanted discharging device, like the solar panel system without the blocking diode.

So what reason would we have for anything more than the basic charging system as described earlier? Let me describe a few!

As long as your battery is near full charge and your load demand is small the 7345 may never be required to deliver all the current that it is capable of delivering. When it is running at partial load, it will not demand the full amount of household current that it normally consumes at full load. And your Honda 1000 will handle it just fine until...you have a discharged battery or you turn 'on' everything that uses 12 volt power. Presto, the Honda trips off line. You reset it. It trips off again. You can't recharge at all! Start the vehicle engine...

You visit your relatives and want to plug into their house power to supply your RV. But they only have a 15 amp duplex outlet for you to use and it is a GFIC outlet with some other things already plugged into it. As soon as you draw more than 5 amps, you trip the breaker in the house. You wear out their circuit breaker as well as your welcome!

You have upgraded to four batteries for dry camping on those long winter evenings in the State Run Campground, where generators are not allowed after 8 p.m. and not before 10 a.m. You anxiously start your generator at 10 a.m. and find you need to run it all day long just to recharge from the previous evening's use. You hang out at the campground all day because you need to gas up the generator and don't want to leave it running unattended. You miss out on the side trip to the waterfalls.

You are a ham radio operator. Every time you turn on your 7345 type converter, you get this horrible buzzing noise on your receiver, particularly on 40 meters. Even when you are using commercial power (no generators) you still have that damn noise...

I have done them all! There is a cure! Read on...

How many places can we get 12 volt charging power? Solar panels, wind turbines, vehicle alternators, converters, crude battery chargers, and from the 12 volt output from some generators.

We have already discussed the basics of solar panels. Panels are unregulated and those over 100 watts which deliver 5 or more amps in full sun and if permanently connected to the battery will need a charge regulator to prevent overcharge. Wind turbines are also unregulated and require not only a charge regulator, but a *diversion load*. When a wind turbine has fully completed its charging job, its excess energy must be forcefully diverted i.e. wasted into a load device like a large resistor to prevent the wind turbine from over-speed mechanical damage. You can't just unplug them, they've always got to be connected to something; we don't want boiling battery water!

Generators like the Honda inverter series have a direct 12 volt charging output. It is unregulated and can climb to 14.5 volts into a light load. Fortunately, the current provided is under 10 amps; it can be treated like a small vehicle alternator. The Hondas have a trap door blocking diode and can be permanently connected to the battery through a suitable 20 amp fuse. Since they only produce 12 volts when the generator is operating, the lack of any regulation is not a problem. Much like a vehicle alternator, they don't run continuously and when they do run the battery usually needs to be charged anyway. I have never observed an overcharge problem from a Honda 12 volt output and have had a Honda 3000 12 volt output connected directly to my coach battery string for 10 years continuously.

Vehicle alternators don't cause overcharge either. There are a number of reasons why. First, they are continuously connected to a chassis battery, which keeps them from exceeding 14.5 volts. Second, the vehicle system is not constantly connected to the trailer (nor in a motor home to the coach battery) nor is the engine run constantly. Third, the charge wire size is small enough and its length long enough to cause significant loss between the vehicle alternator and the coach battery. This loss limits the total available charging current to the coach battery to something like 20 amps, except in large Class A motor homes which use a controlled bridging solenoid system.

Plain old crude battery chargers are usually capable of no more than 10 amps and are also unregulated. Generally we only use a crude battery charger on a dead battery and it is connected with large clamps and only temporarily. A crude battery charger IS capable of overcharging a battery if it is left connected past when the battery is fully recharged.

Converters come in two basic configurations: Linear power supplies (those with huge heavy power transformers) and switching power supplies (the light ones commonly found factory installed in most RVs.) Switching power supplies can further be subdivided into models that have intelligent battery charging and maintenance algorithms (intelligent converters) and plain regulated converters (those which supply a fixed output voltage regardless of load.) Linear power supplies are much heavier per amp delivered than are switching converters. Linear converters are much less efficient (only about 60% of the energy consumed is output as useful charging power) than switching converters (nearly 85% of the energy consumed is useful as output charging current.)

Linear converters do have one important advantage over switching converters. They produce virtually no electromagnetic interference (EMI). Switching converters by their very operation produce EMI that is detectable in sensitive radio receivers, particularly in low noise environments like a wide open country campground. This EMI seems to always be the most severe in the 7 Mhz range but affects all MF and HF frequencies to some degree. Even the most modern and sophisticated switching converters suffer from this malady to some extent. If you must have the best possible signal to noise ratio in a receiver, the inefficient linear converter is a must have.

Both linear and switching converters come in assorted amperage capacities. Linear supplies are always larger and heavier in similar capacities.

Commonly available RV switching supplies are 35,45,60,and 80 amps. Commonly available linear supplies are 20,30,40,and 50 amps.

Switching supplies are almost always fused and always trap door (blocking diode) protected. RV switching supplies have no user control over output voltage, although some models made for non-RV battery elimination purposes have such user controls.

Linear supplies are not inherently designed for RV use. They are converter dinosaurs; scaled down versions of what the telephone company has used for decades. They have no output fusing and usually no trap door circuitry. In fact, many models can be ruined by connecting them to a battery since they are designed to be used as a battery substitute. These problems can be overcome as I will show you later with a modified Astron supply. Linear supplies also offer precise control over the output voltage as well as current limiting.

Too Many Choices?

In the simple charging system diagrammed earlier, the RV manufacturer usually picks a switching converter based on the number of batteries in the coach system. More accurately the converter minimum size should really be chosen based on the amp hour capacity of the combined battery string.

For example, a group 27 12 volt car battery (about 90 amp hours) should have a minimum of a 35 amp converter. A string of two of these batteries or two golf cart batteries (180 and 225 amp hours respectively) should have at least a 55 to 60 amp converter. A Class A with a pair of 4D's should have at least an 80 amp converter.

Note we are talking minimum charging capacity for a working RV. As noted earlier, a group 27 can be harmlessly float charged forever with a 500ma unregulated solar panel, just enough to make it survive. A group of four batteries or a couple of 4d's can be harmlessly float charged with a regulated 100 watt solar panel, (about 5 amps peak).

But we have not discussed MAXIMUM charge rates. Lead-acid and AGM batteries can be recharged at much higher rates than what our RV manufacturer supplied. Consider a car alternator. Most modern pickups have a 140 amp alternator and a single group 27 battery. WOW. Why would they put such a huge charging system on that battery? Because of all the lights and toys we now have in our vehicles. It all adds up. It wouldn't do for our car to stop running because we turned the stereo system up too loud.

But when that stereo is turned off, the full 140 amps is available to charge the battery. And that much charging power can recharge a dead car battery double quick, in about 20 minutes from flat dead!

So why should we wait all day to recharge our dead RV battery? The only thing slowing us down is the converter! If you do the math you can see that if it is safe to recharge a group 27 car battery with 140 amps it is safe to recharge at pair of 4d's with 4x140=560 amps! Now I don't know anyone with a 560 amp converter! But if we can *discharge* such a battery string with an inverter with a couple of microwaves on high (sucking 400 amps from the battery) we can certainly replace that charge at the same rate. Our old friends at the telephone company have been doing this for years. The same technology was used to power those World War II diesel/electric submarines. The telephone company can easily draw 3000 amps at 48 volts during afternoon rush hour. They simply have 15 each 300 amp converters to keep up with it and with their 10,000 amp hour battery capacity, they can recharge in about 2 hours from flat dead. Damn the torpedoes, etc.

Now I am not suggesting that we all run out and buy 560 amp converters. Even if we could safely vent the hydrogen during such a recharge, where would we find 75 amps of 120 volt household current to satisfy our greedy converter? I don't haul around a 10KW generator and most of you don't either. But I am saying that if properly vented, such a string could be safely recharged at that rate from dead flat in about an hour.

Now if it takes about five amps to keep that string of four alive and we can force 560 amps into them in a pinch that leaves a lot of room in the middle. To give us that kind of flexibility we need proper venting, proper wire sizing, and the right combination of converters.

Why would we want four batteries? Many of my clients use large inverters so they can live normal TV watching lives at night when dry camping. Some like to run room air conditioners in their bedrooms at night off of battery power. Some just like large tailgate parties with no generator noise with no hookups available.

I settle for a compromise, using four batteries, a 100 watt regulated solar panel, 12 amps from my running Honda, up to 30 amps from my truck charging line, and four converters of various sizes. The top recharge rate I can get from all the converters is about 150 amps.

The primary converter is a Progressive Dynamics PD9260 with charge wizard. This one is on the main shore power 30 amp feed. It is always on, float charging the batteries, along with the solar panel. Since I store my rig covered, the solar panel rarely puts out more than two amps, leaving the battery charging chores to the 9260 when the rig is stored. The 9260 is an intelligent converter. It knows when I am using the rig and adjusts up its charging voltage to 13.6. It knows when I am not using the rig for 12 hours and drops back to a 13 volt float to avoid overcharging. And once a month it jumps into boost mode and forces 14.5 volts into the string for 12 hours to desulfate the plates. I check the water annually and add a slight amount. My batteries are still at 70 percent capacity after seven years of age, when I replace them. The Charge Wizard forces the 9260 through its modes manually should I want to. This converter charges at 60 amps maximum and draws 9.6 amps of household power at full output.

My second converter is a Parallax Power 7345. It puts out 13.7 volts at up to 45 amps, drawing a maximum of 7.3 amps of household power. It was chosen to match to the Honda 3000is because it can run at full output drawing its 7.3 amp maximum along with a 15,000 btu air conditioner running at full cool drawing 13.5 amps. These two units together draw about 21 amps, which is a full load for the 3000is.

My third and fourth converters are linear converters. The smaller converter is a homemade 11 amp linear converter with a cut-off relay for trap door capability. The relay is in the output circuit and disconnects the converter from the battery when the converter is powered down. It is for park use when I want very low EMI charging while operating my radio equipment. It can also serve as a stand-alone charger in situations where only 3 amps of household power can be spared for my use. This 11 amps, plus the 6 amp solar panel peak output can sustain my dry camping needs if necessary. The float voltage on the linear converters is adjusted to 13.5 volts.

The fourth converter is a modified Astron RM-50M linear power supply. It is modified with a cut-off relay and has been modified for adjustable current limiting. This supply is used for high current charging in an EMI free environment, such as ARRL Field Day. Since the Astron is rated at 50 amps peak only, the current has to be limited to 40 amps in continuous usage. Modification details are available from the Astron website. The float voltage is adjusted to 13.5 volts so it comes online after the switching supplies when used in combination. A trap door relay is installed in the output line.

These last three converters may be selected in any combination through the use of a power strip, which has been modified with 20 amp SPST relays, which energize individual outlets on the strip. These 12 volt relays are energized by a rotary switch inside the coach. All neutrals are isolated for reasons explained elsewhere in this book.

Chapter 4

Shore Power Feeds

If we are using four selectable converters, two room air conditioners, (in addition to the rooftop unit), a washer/dryer, multiple TV sets, and kitchen appliances, we can't possibly expect a feeble 30 amp RV service plug to meet our household current needs.

So I have developed methods to split my current demand so that I can fully exploit any available current source from a lowly 5 amp 120VAC outlet all the way up to dual 50 amp 120VAC park service.

As explained in detail in my first book, I use a large inverter to supply 120VAC to my rig when insufficient amperage is available to satisfy the normal non-air-conditioned day-to-day load. Since my first book was written, I have substituted a Samlex 4000 watt true sinusoidal inverter for the Portawattz 3000 MSW inverter I used in 2005. This was done to reduce EMI for the sake of my radio receivers, and it helps significantly.

The same 2005 transfer switching arrangement is still in use, as is shown in Diagram 13 of my first book. I still automatically transfer three circuits on the original shore power panel to the inverter whenever the inverter is powered on. I also still have two circuits on the original main panel that do not transfer, "shore only". I still have an additional 50 amp inverter powered relay in my transfer relay box that transfers the rooftop air conditioner from the original main panel to the generator output. This single relay can now also be switched on manually using power from the original main power panel.

I have added additional separate circuit duplex outlets around the coach with their own isolated feed arrangement. Also new are two 30 amp main circuit breakers, fed by #10 drop cord pigtails in the basement. One breaker feeds the transferred rooftop air conditioner (A/C CKT) circuit and the other feeds the isolated outlets and the converter selector power strip described earlier (CHG CKT). I 'plug up' the rig differently depending on the available power source(s).

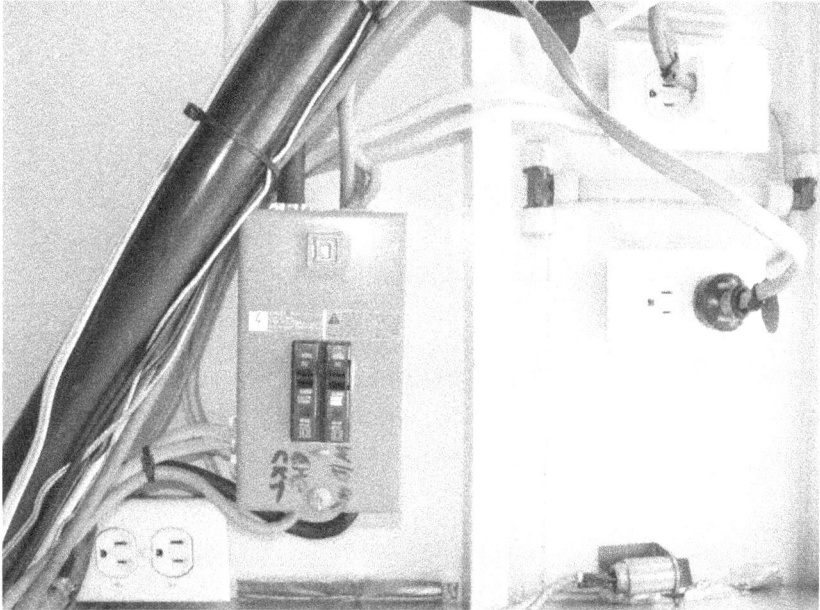

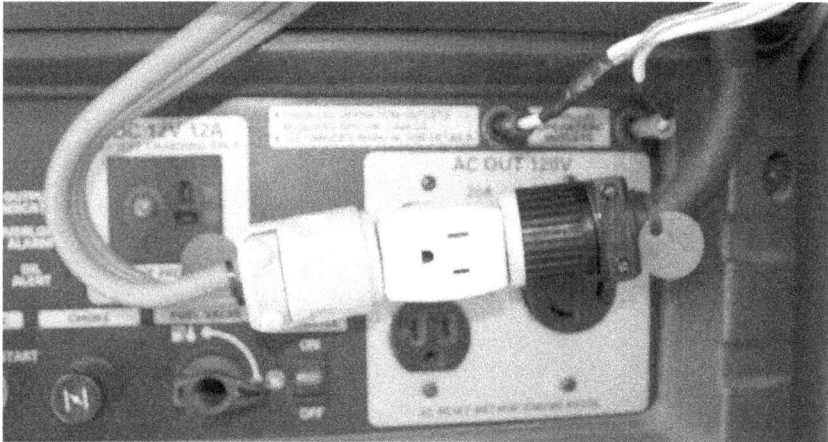

The two #10 pigtails are shown plugged into the generator, as they would be for dry camping. These pigtails feed the circuit breaker (top picture). Neutrals are isolated; grounds are common. The W/D A/C CKT feeds the 50 amp transfer relay make contacts as well as separate duplex outlets throughout the rig. The CHG CKT feeds the converter power strip and other neutral isolated duplex outlets elsewhere in the rig living room and bedroom via the pictured duplex outlets at the right. The CHG CKT circuit outlets are labeled.

Dry Camping

When dry camping, the only available power is what you make yourself. My dry camping power source is a Honda EU3000is and a Honda 2000. As you see above, the Honda 3000 feeds the CHG CKT and the W/D A/C CKT. Since the inverter is operating when dry camping, the W/D A/C CKT is transferred to the generator from the main shore power feed. Therefore the circuits to the washer/dryer and the rooftop air conditioner work only when the Honda 3000 is running. All other outlets and circuits except 'shore only' circuits are power by the inverter. The converter selector is set to use the Magnetek 7345. Therefore when we start the generator it will charge the battery bank at 45 amps (plus whatever the solar panel is producing plus about 15 amps from the Honda's 12 volt charger. This is sufficient to keep the batteries charged while simultaneously using the inverter to supply all other needs. This scheme works up to about 5000 feet of elevation, above which the Honda 3000 is gasping for air, and can only power the rooftop air conditioner alone.

The Honda 2000 is used to supply the room air conditioners via the separate wiring when extra cooling is needed.

These EXT PLUG outlets are wired through the coachwork using #14 drop cords (3 conductor extension cord with the female end cut off). The cut off end is wired to the outlet; each male end is in the basement near the generator. The bedroom and living room EXT PLUG outlets are shown above plugged into the basement CHG CKT duplex outlets. When used with the Honda 2000, they are unplugged in the basement and routed via extension cord to the Honda 2000 placed nearby outside. This supplies power to the EXT PLUG outlets in the rig living room and bedroom (pictured below.)

The room air conditioners are plugged in to the EXT PLUG outlets and therefore receive their power from the Honda 2000 directly. The room air conditioners can also be plugged into nearby household outlets and operated by the inverter should you want room air conditioning after hours when generators are not allowed. Since they draw about 5 amps each (50 amps from the battery) a single room air conditioner will run about eight hours on a string of four batteries.

At higher altitude, the Honda 3000 will not be able to run the 7345 converter and the rooftop air conditioner simultaneously. You must therefore settle for the 15 to 20 amps provided by the Honda 12 volt charger and the solar panel when you want the air conditioner to operate. In this case we can unplug the CHG CKT from the Honda 3000 and route it to the Honda 2000 outside. We then select the charging rate that matches our other Honda 2000 demands.

If we don't need rooftop air conditioning we can just shut off the Honda 3000 and use the Honda 2000 to charge the batteries via the CHG CKT plug up. This results in very low gas consumption of about 1 gallon per day to provide all electricity needs (inverter 'on'.) We can place the 2000 away from our rig and use an extension cord.

I use such a setup also when I want very low EMI. Placing the generator far away greatly reduces RF noise. I use the Astron RM50 50 amp linear converter only and a Corcom 30EMC6 30 amp common mode line filter (see below) at the generator.

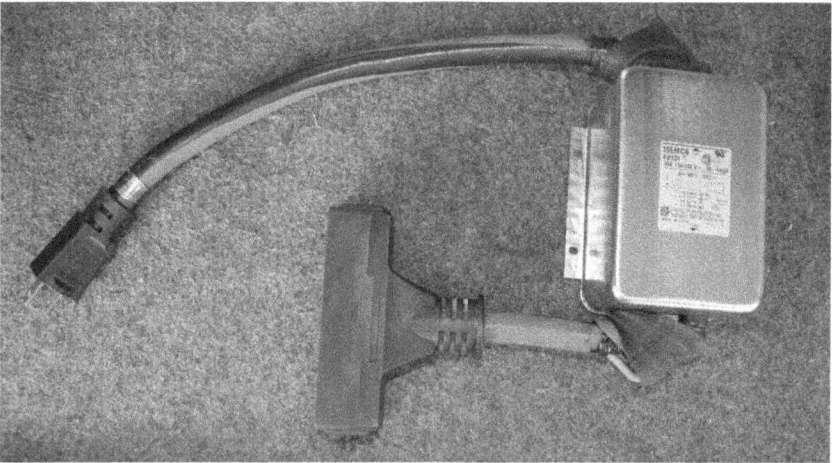

For the More Daring...

The following loads are placed on the 'shore only' circuit breakers in the original main panel and would not normally be used dry camping: The electric water heater circuit (if equipped); the built in converter (in my case an Intellipower PD9260), the electric space heater, and the AC section of the refrigerator. In each case these functions are replaced by their propane equivalents while dry camping. The converting job is done with the other converters.

Notwithstanding, it is possible to have the inverter running and back feed the original main panel via the regular shore power cable from the Honda 2000. Since the 'shore only' loads are never transferred and the other loads are already transferred, The Honda can power these shore only loads if necessary. For safety reasons I shut off the transferred load circuit breakers in the original main service panel when I attempt this. That way if the inverter is inadvertently shut off, it cannot damage itself by momentary shorting across the generator's voltage as the various relay contacts open.

Less Than 30 Amps Available

Whenever available current is less than standard 30 amp RV service, I energize the inverter and 'run everything' off of the inverter. I am still not using the main 30 amp RV shore cord. I plug up the CHG CKT cord to the available household current supply. The reason I just 'give up' on using a substandard power source is the annoyance of having the power fail unpredictably throughout the day and potential damage from low voltage. The inverter never fails.

I then use a converter of my choice to keep the battery charged as explained above, choosing a converter or combination of converters that will not overload the available current supply. Obviously under these meager situations, the rooftop air conditioner cannot be used unless I power up the Honda 3000. I can however use a single 5000 BTU room air conditioner, powered from the available supply current, or at night from the inverter if necessary. When using a room air conditioner on the meager supply, I reduce the converter draw by selecting a smaller converter to relieve enough capacity to supply the 5 to 7 amps needed by the room air conditioner.

30 Amp Park Power

Well, we have finally made it to an RV park with a real power plug. I have long since discarded my 30 amp RV plug on the shore cord and replaced it with a conventional standard 20 amp plug. In 20 years of camping I have never overheated or had trouble with a 20 amp standard plug supplying 30 amps to my rig. And it's way easier to plug in at home for storage. So I have made up an adapter to convert my cord *back up* to the standard 30 amp RV receptacle. Such adapters are inexpensive and available at Camping World.

Basically, we just plug in to the 30 amp service with our shore cord. We do have to manage our power consumption. We don't need to use our inverter. We do need to monitor the supplied line voltage since many parks still have inferior wiring.

Typically I try to run the refrigerator on AC power, and avoid using the washer/dryer when the rooftop air conditioner is on. There may be enough power to run the electric water heater, but avoid it while cooking meals. The microwave and the air conditioner together may be too much for the circuit. Use of additional room air conditioners is out of the question. Try to cook outside. Life is good.

30 Plus 20 GFI Power

Most parks that have a 30 amp plug will have a 20 amp GFI plug right next to it. How many of us have tried to use both and failed! Well, with our setup we finally have it licked! Imagine nearly 50 amps available for the price of 30! Some parks watch you and forbid multiple power cords and power adapters outright. Most parks look the other way as long as you don't cause them trouble. Most novice campers who try to use both plugs just trip the GFI and give up on the idea, making the park operators happy. And it's not even the camper's fault!

Typical Park Plug

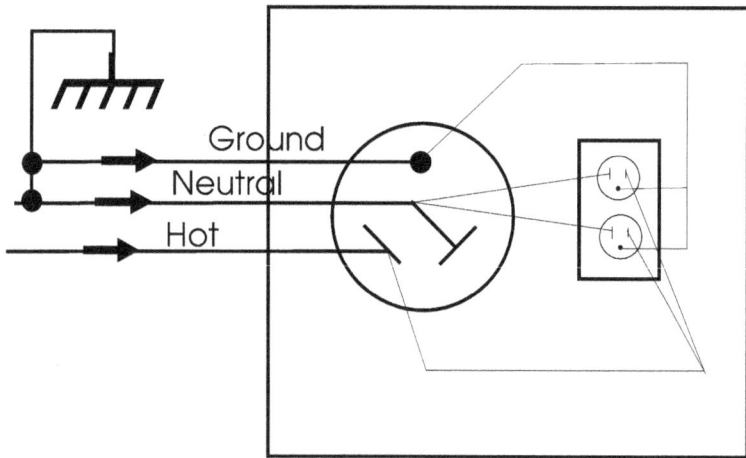

The reason most people trip the GFI on the 20 amp side because of the design of the park power plug. Notice from the drawing above that the ground and neutral leads are common to both plugs The circuit breakers are not shown for each plug in the drawing above, but the hot leads are also common when the breakers are closed. The real cause of the problem is with the ground and the neutral, which are bonded at the utility service entrance to the park, just as they are bonded at the service entrance to your house. The only real source of a safety ground is that ground rod at the service entrance. The utility itself provides no safety ground.

So we happily plug into the 30 amp side of the service. This connects hot and neutral to our rig and also grounds our rig to that quasi-ground being provided by the park, just for our safety of course! That park ground is bonded to the park neutral. So our rig ground is also bonded to our rig neutral. Now I will argue that the park ground is so far away from our rig that it really is not a good ground anyway, and we should have our own ground rod, but that is food for another book. Anyway, our rig has a ground fault provided free by the park!

So we decide to run one of our circuits from the park 20 amp GFI. But we wire the plug to share the same ground and the same neutral, using the hot lead as an extra power source. Sharing the neutral should work fine, after all we share our neutral throughout our home on all circuits. (More on shared neutrals later.) It's always okay to share the ground, but if we share a neutral on our rig, the GFI sees that park provided ground fault and trips. And that ground fault is coming from the park ground bonding feeding back through our own 30 amp plug neutral. So we have to make a choice, plug into the 20 or plug into the 30 but not both.

Another caveat is that many inverters also bond their neutral output to the chassis ground of the inverter. As if an inverter chassis was of any use as a ground. This introduces another possible ground fault generated within our rig.

The only sure fire way to avoid tripping that 20 amp GFI is to make sure that anything plugged in to it has a neutral that is COMPLETELY ISOLATED from our rig neutral. The wiring on my EXT PLUG and CHG CKT meet just that criteria. The neutral and hot leads are completely isolated from the rig main service panel, only sharing grounds.

So we plug up our CHG CKT into the GFI. We have our own 30 amp breaker on the hot lead, and we route the neutral through and share it with nothing except our isolated EXT PLUGs and the converter switched power strip. Typically what I use this extra 20 amps for is to operate the room air conditioners and to charge my battery, relieving my 30 amp main panel for other duties like heating water or running an electric heater. I even have an EXT PLUG near my washer/dryer, so I can use the extra power to dry clothes. The only limitation is to make sure any appliance you plug in doesn't have a ground fault of its own. You are always safe if the device you plug in has a three prong plug.

It is also a good idea to monitor the line voltage on both the 30 and the 20 amp feed. Sometimes you will draw enough current to pull the voltage down to unsafe levels: under 104 volts. It is also necessary to use a #10 wire gauge extension cord for the CHG CKT feed to keep voltage drop to a minimum.

I always try to disguise the dual feeds so as to not alarm the park police. Using nice large short extension cords that go directly into the coach is much better than having small orange wires and power strips outside. That stuff is unsafe and will raise the red flag.

50 Amp Top of the Line Service

So how much more can you ask for than 30 plus 20? Well, 50 plus 50 of course! You will probably have to pay more for this type service but if it's really hot or cold outside, it's worth it.

We had left Amarillo on our way to the Metroplex and decided to pull into Vernon for the evening. It was July and blazing hot as only Texas can be in the summer. We grabbed a pull through site since we planned to leave early in the morning for Arlington. We hooked up to the 50 amp service and were excited to be able to cool down for the evening. A nice dip in the pool and off to bed.

I awakened at 7 a.m. as the power surged and the air conditioners shut down. Funny thing, the converter was charging, but the microwave light was out. The main TV was OK and DirecTv was on. A faint smell of burning electric filled the air. Not Good.

My permanent metering showed zero volts on feed B and 240 volts on feed A. I rushed outside and unplugged my rig from the park supply. I grabbed a meter and measured the voltage at the park box. The plug showed 240 volts across the feeds but only 10 volts from the feeds to the neutral. Oh Nooo…

The park neutral wire had burned itself open. Since the park was using 240 center tapped, my air conditioner load pulled feed B to ground, forcing 240 into the side A feed. As the park owner calmly repaired his substandard #10 neutral I was burning up angry, knowing that he had caused me at least $3000 in damage in an instant.

Since I repair RV's myself, I was forced to spend my next two vacation days repairing the damage: Blown microwave, blown refer heating element, blown Samsung BluRay player, blown bedroom TV, blown VCR, ruined cordless drill charger, etc. etc. Fortunately I have dealer accounts and was able to find everything locally at cost in the Dallas area.

The folks in Texas are very nice, but I didn't leave the state until the park owner's insurance check was in hand.…

As you can see this is a study in what not to do if you are an RV park. Most parks provide 240 center tapped service at 50 amp outlets, just like is provided to your home by the power company. The big difference is that RV's do not have any 240 volt appliances and are never in need of 240 volt service. The proper way to feed a 50 amp RV plug is with 120 volts to each feed with an oversized neutral. That way if the neutral ever should open, everything would safely shut down and never be force fed 240 VAC. Very few parks do this properly, so you are advised to inspect the hookup well and beware of parks that have hookups like those pictured above. If you are going to take risks then I advise you to invest in a Surge Guard 34750-001 for $450.

My rig was never intended to use 50 amp service; it shipped with 30 amp service to a single service panel. Rigs with 50 amp service have dual sided service panels with loads distributed evenly between the A and the B feed to a common neutral. Most shore power cord neutral wires are the same gauge as the A and B feed wires, generally #8 or #6 drop cord. These cords are massive and hard to handle but the large gauge wire is essential for carrying 50 amps. We already know that voltage drop from using undersized extension cords is a big problem with RVs. Using an undersize neutral not only causes voltage drop, it causes overheat and eventual failure as well.

I have already described how to add additional EXT PLUG outlets to your rig at selected locations where you intend to use an appliance like a room air conditioner or electric space heater. I also rearranged my original main panel to isolate the 'shore only' loads from the loads that I transfer to the inverter. I also added a high current (50 amp) transfer relay that will transfer the washer/dryer and the rooftop air conditioner from the main panel to the generator via the W/D A/C CKT 30 amp breaker.

When I use a 50 amp park supply, I use a special adapter cord. This cord splits the dual feeds into a single 'A' feed and two bridged 'B' feeds.

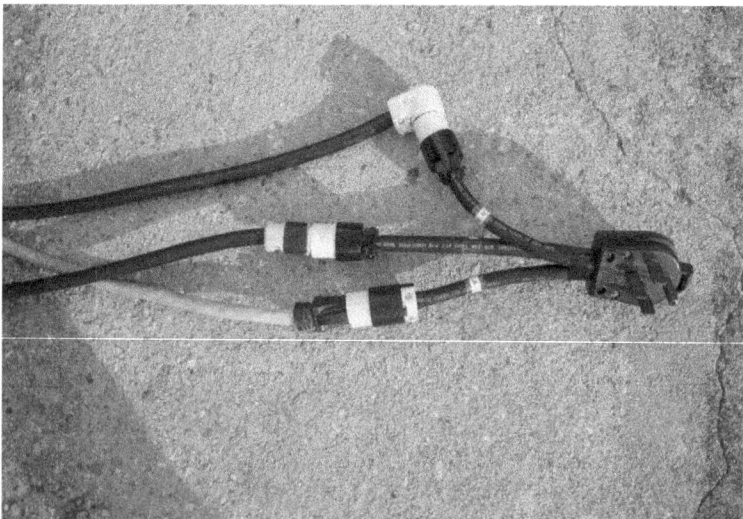

At the top of the picture is the 'A' feed which is plugged into the rig main shore power cord, a #10 drop cord. The bottom two are #10 extension cords that are routed through a basement access hole to the W/D A/C plug and the CHG CKT plug. Of course these two are unplugged from the generator where they are normally left while traveling.

The adapter plug is pictured below. It is made up of common electrical parts found at Home Depot. Make sure to use 20 amp drop cord receptacle caps and #10 drop cord for the assembly.

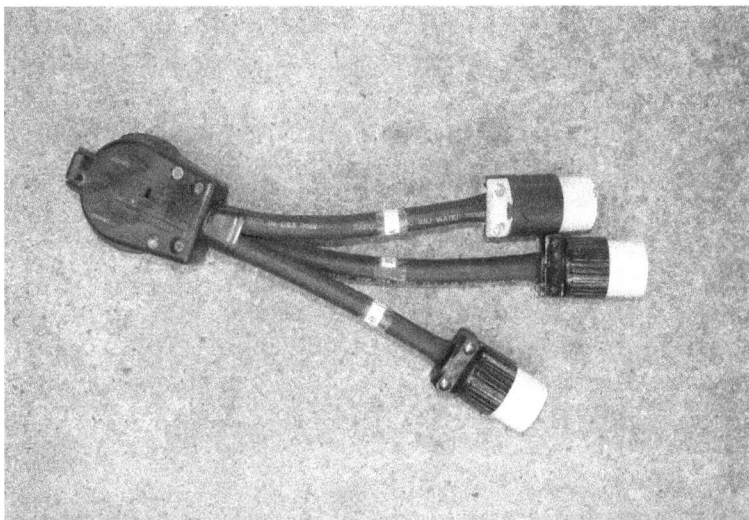

I have a toggle switch that allows me to manually close the 50 amp W/D A/C transfer relay. It is a SPDT switch that in position one allows inverter generated 120 VAC to operate the relay. The switch is normally left in this position. That way when the inverter is turned on, the inverter will operate the relay, transferring the W/D A/C to the generator. And when the inverter is off, the relay is off and the W/D A/C operate from the main shore panel circuit. In position two the relay coil is connected directly to 120 VAC from the main panel. Thus when the shore power cord is connected, the relay is operated, also transferring the W/D A/C to the generator. But alas we have unplugged this feed from the generator and plugged it in to feed 'B1' of the 50 amp adapter.

The CHG CKT has also been moved from the generator to feed 'B2' of the 50 amp adapter. We also plug the washer/dryer, living room and bedroom EXT PLUGs into the CHG CKT outlets in the basement.

This plug up arrangement provides 3 separate #10 feeds to the rig, capable of carrying a combined 100 amps safely, 33 amps per feed. The combined wire gauge of three number ten wires is better than the equivalent of a single number six wire (commonly found on 50 amp rigs). The combined neutrals are also equivalent of #6 or better (5½ to be exact), making this arrangement stronger and safer than even the largest OEM 50 amp RV shore power cords found in use today. And it is much easier to handle and store three smaller power cords than one massive one. In addition, you may be able to use a shorter cord for the 'B' feeds (depending on the location of the park plug) reducing extension cord power losses even further.

It is important to use 20 amp rated plugs and receptacle caps on these cords, even though they cost more than commonly available 15 amp plug materials. Home Depot and most hardware stores carry what you need. The #10 drop cord can be purchased by the foot. I make up my own extension cords, and carry none other than #10 gauge cords, 1-7 footer, 1-15 footer, and 1-50 footer. This allows me to use the shortest amount of cord necessary to reach the park plug.

So let's summarize our feeds. Feed 'A' is fed to the RV main service panel, supplying the electric water heater, the refrigerator, one of the thermostatically installed electric space heaters and the main converter (if we choose to use it) via the 'shore only' circuit breakers. It also supplies the microwave oven and the convenience outlets throughout the rig for the bedroom and entertainment centers, as supplied by the manufacturer, through their respective breakers on the main panel. Total current: Varies from 15 to 35 amps.

Since we have operated our toggle switch, we have the washer/dryer, the rooftop air conditioner, and the second thermostatically controlled electric heater powered through feed 'B1', drawing a maximum of 25 amps. Obviously we don't use the air conditioners and the space heaters simultaneously. This circuit is protected by a 30 amp main breaker only.

We have plugged feed 'B2' into the CHG CKT line and via the EXT PLUG's, we can operate our two room air conditioners, the converter power strip, the decorative electric fireplace, and the George Forman Electric Grill. Total draw is 20 to 30 amps. This circuit too is protected by a 30 amp main breaker only.

So we have the convenience of total electric living, using propane only for occasional cooking. We also need supplemental propane heat if the outside temperature falls below 20°F. Livin' large.

The 15,000 BTU Coleman Mach roof top air conditioner (14 amps full draw) plus two 5000 BTU window mounted room air conditioners (5 amps each) will cool the 300 square foot rig interior to 32°F lower than the outside ambient temperature parked in full sun. Daytime in Dallas it was 70° inside and 104° outside, day after day. Daytime temperatures only cooled to below 100°F outside when we crested Pacheco Pass heading west toward home.

I inspect all my connections daily and can report no problems with overheating plugs. I have had trouble with overheated 15 amp plugs in the past. I monitor both the 'A' and the 'B' feed line voltages constantly with built-in metering.

Ground Faults and the Common Neutral

As you remember, the park provides us with a free ground fault when we plug into their power. This can cause a real nuisance to big rig owners with 50 amp rigs if they were to attempt to split the 30-20 service of lesser parks.

I had a summer service call to the Seventh Day Adventist campground on Old San Jose Road. It seems this guy with a brand new high end fifth wheel had half of his appliances not working. What to do? Camp was just starting up and he was going to spend the whole week with half a rig?

When I arrived I found he had a dual feed 50 amp panel and that indeed one side of his panel was dead. Upon further investigation, I found he was trying to run his rig off a 30 amp park plug and was using an inexpensive moulded adapter which converted the 30 amp service to his 50 amp plug. Unfortunately the adapter was only supplying 120 VAC to only one side of his 50 amp feed plug. I went to the hardware store and bought a 50 amp receptacle and a box to mount it in. I cut off the 50 amp end of the adapter and wired the pigtail into the new box and receptacle, feeding both A and B with the single 30 amp hot wire. It solved the problem. I warned the customer not to use too many appliances at the same time as he might trip the park breaker. All was well.

Was the adapter defective or was it designed that way? No one can tell but it probably has to do with the idea that a user could overheat the #10 adapter cord if both feeds were used and they might sue....

So when you buy 50 amp adapters, take an ohmeter along so you can see exactly what you are getting. It might be the shaft. And so what does this have to do with ground faults anyway?

Well, the creative 50 amp RV owner might have the grand idea that he could plug into a 30-20GFI park plug and get power from each to feed his 50 amp dual A and B feed. All he needs is the correct adapter, right? After all, the neutrals are common, the grounds are common, and we just have two hot wires for A and B. This is too good to be true! So he buys a 50 amp receptacle and a box to house it. He buys two pieces of drop cord and a 20 amp 120 VAC plug for the GFI and a 30 amp male RV plug for the 30 amp side. He connects both green wires in the box to the ground lug. He connects both white wires to the neutral lug. And finally he wires one black wire to the 'A' feed and the other black wire to the 'B' feed. Finished.

He plugs his rig into the receptacle on his custom adapter. He plugs the 30 amp side in. No problem. He plugs the 20 amp GFI in. It trips. Why?

If he unplugs his rig and tries again it still trips! The park's own ground fault is tripping the GFI outlet. So he gets creative and disconnects the ground to the 30 amp side. It still trips. The neutral is still common and the ground from the GFI outlet itself will cause it to trip! How do we solve this dilemma?

There is no way. If we disconnect the ground from the park 30 amp as well as from the park 20 amp GFI, it will still trip. The GFI is connected to the park ground inside the box and uses it for a reference. As long as our load neutrals are common, the GFI will see the park ground fault. Even if we try to just use the hot lead from the GFI, it will trip due to imbalance. Aren't building codes wonderful? We're just trying to use the power we are paying for. So unless you remove the park GFI outlet and install a normal duplex outlet, you are out of luck with a 50 amp dual feed panel. And I don't recommend messing with the park's outlets, especially if you plan to hold them liable for wreaking havoc on your electrical system.

The whole problem with this (besides the gawd-awful GFI) is the fact that the 50 amp RV panel uses a common neutral for both feeds. If you take off the cover and look you will find that for every load circuit the white neutral wires are on a common bus. And all the bare ground wires are on their own separate common bus. And to make matters worse, that neutral common bus has only one large white neutral feed wire coming from the shore cord.

So unless you are willing to add EXT PLUGs with their own isolated neutral, or to modify your 50 amp panel loads onto two isolated neutral buses with two isolated shore power cords, you will not be able to avail yourself of the 30-20GFI option.

Conclusion

It can become daunting to remember all these complicated methods of plugging in your rig. Along with flexibility comes complexity. One RV repair buddy of mine lamented as he looked on "I would never be able to work on your rig. It's so complex I could never figure it out." He's right. But most RV repairmen are not as creative as we are, and many of us would never let a repairman work on our rig anyway.

After you get used to your rig, these plug in arrangements become second nature. But in any case I use cheat sheets to remind me. I have a written page for each of the highlighted plug-in arrangements outlined above. I just pull out the appropriate sheet depending on the park power available. I also have a quick reference card that shows the basics of each power situation on a single sheet.

Chapter 5

Inside the Rig

The first thing I set up after parking and connecting to the hookups (if any) is the TV. Park cable TV seems to be stuck in the stone age and is obsolete but I always try it anyway just to see how bad it really is. The conversion to digital television has left it in the dust. In many areas, perfectly good high definition TV is available off the air.

The Winegard batwing antenna of old serves just fine in the digital TV environment. Winegard makes an accessory called a 'Wingman' that really does slightly improve reception. It is essentially a 2 element UHF director for the main amplified antenna. The Wingman must be pointed toward the TV station; the standard batwing is bi-directional, meaning it works just as well broadside from its back or its front. Since the batwing mount does not have a full 360° of rotation, it may not be possible to get the unidirectional Wingman perfectly aligned at the station. Fortunately, it is not so critical that 20° of misdirection will matter much. But having it off by 180° will matter a lot. Draw an arrow inside on the antenna azimuth bezel by the crank to show you which way the Wingman is pointed.

Explore the new digital off-air TV environment! If old analog TV was available in the area before, the chances are good that you will now get the digital equivalent. Most stations have also added additional sub-channels to their offerings. Digital TV signal strength seems to be nearly as good as the old analog TV was. But digital either comes in perfectly or checkerboards into blue silence. This can make antenna alignment a guessing game. Some digital TV's have a signal strength menu feature but this feature is usually difficult to interpret. That leaves us to trial and guess unless we know about where the TV transmitting tower is located. In spite of the antenna pointing problems, local research will make the results worthwhile.

I also recommend ditching your old TV and going to flat screens. Don't waste money on digital converters. The new digital picture quality is superb. I will show you some installation tips later.

Dish Location and Setup

Many RVers now use satellite TV service. I have had both Dish Network and DirecTv. Dish alignment on Dish Network is easier than DirecTv, but Dish Network doesn't work well in northern Mexico and seems to have an inferior channel lineup offering.

Dish versus Direct also presents us with the need to use incompatible dish antenna hardware. This can lead to significant expense if you have a permanent dome installation and choose to change providers, or to upgrade to HDTV. In addition, permanent dome installations are maintenance intensive. They also have the disadvantage of not working when you park under a tree. I am not a fan of domes and prefer to set up my own tripod at my campsite.

It does take a few minutes to set up a tripod and dish. You also have to select a site for the dish with an unobstructed view to the south. This still offers more flexibility than you get with a dome.

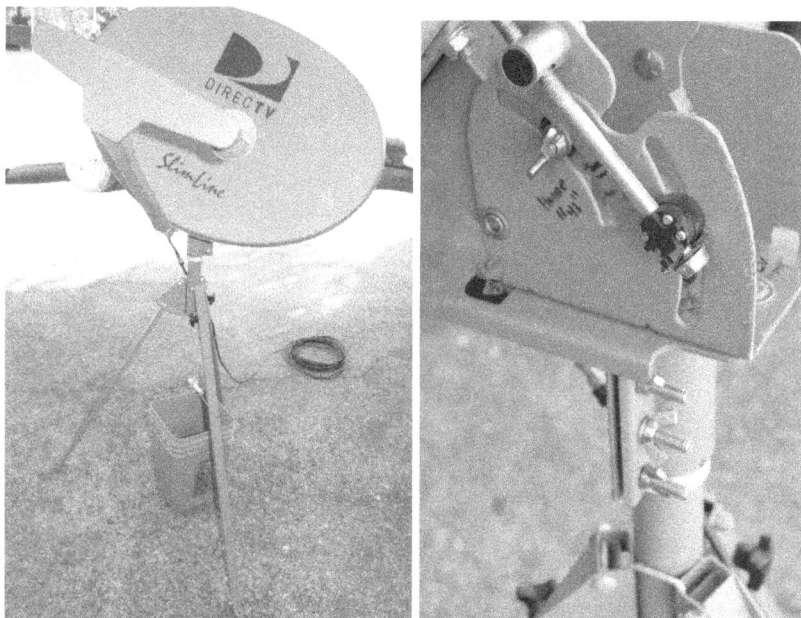

The tripod I prefer is the Winegard TR-3535. I hang a bucket of water under it for stability when I can't stake it down. The feet holes need to be drilled out to 3/8 inch to accept standard tent stakes. In addition, the mast is only 1 9/16 in outside diameter. While this is ideal for small dishes it is too small for the DirecTv Slimline, which requires a 2 inch OD mast. This problem is easily solved by using a 6 inch long piece of 1½ inch schedule 40 PVC pipe. The pipe piece is notched along its full length with a saw. It is then pried open slightly and pushed onto the mast. It makes a nice snug fit, but you can epoxy it on if you like. The result, pictured below makes a perfect fit for a Slimline dish.

It is absolutely essential that the bubble (inserted in the top of the mast) correctly reads perfect plumb. It is a plastic insert and is usually incorrect as shipped. Using a torpedo level, set up the tripod perfectly plumb, measuring on the outside of the PVC in many places. When you are satisfied, epoxy the bubble insert in place, making sure the bubble reads exactly in the center of the circle. Pry up around the edges of the insert until you are satisfied; recheck your mast with the torpedo level. Then leave it alone to dry.

The Slimline dish should be bought locally from a DirecTv installer or can be obtained via the internet with increased cost due to shipping. It will come complete with LNB head and a single stub of RG6 coaxial cable about 18 inches long. Note that I have upgraded the mounting hardware to 5/16 inch stainless steel carriage bolts with wing nuts on the mast and elevation notches. This allows mounting and rough adjustment without the use of tools.

The dish is connected to the satellite receiver with a length of up to 200 feet of RG6 cable, the same stuff used by the cable TV company. It can be bought at Home Depot by the foot. The Slimline LNB requires 18 to 20 volts to operate, more than the 15 volts supplied by a receiver. You will need to obtain a DirecTv 21V SWM Power Inserter (PI21, available for about $15). This is connected between the receiver and the dish, and requires 120 VAC to operate.

To set up the dish, first turn on your TV and go into the satellite setup menu. You will need the zip code (or latitude and longitude) of your current location. Enter this info into the setup program and the receiver will display the heading (azimuth), elevation, and skewing angle for your location. The heading displayed is in magnetic degrees so you do not need to fool with declination conversion calculations.

For example, my location in California calls for 124° azimuth, 42° skewing, and 62° elevation. I use a hand-bearing compass (Weems and Plath 2004-S) and locate an object on the horizon at 124°. Less expensive compasses can be used, but I like to be finished quickly and instrument precision within 3° is important. You will want a location for your tripod that has no sky clutter (read tree branches) within 20° left and right of your azimuth number, and no clutter within 10° up and down of your elevation number.

Set up your tripod and get it absolutely plumb, using the bubble. Tighten the legs and stake it down. Set the dish onto the mast. Using the numbers engraved on the dish, set the skewing and elevation to the values for your location. Later fine tuning of the skewing is not necessary, so just tighten it down now.

Stand behind the dish with your hand-bearing compass and find an object on the horizon at your heading. Look down at the mounting bracket and up at the object. Swing the dish to your best guess of alignment with the mounting bracket. Snug up the wing nuts so that the dish no longer droops on the mast. Recheck your bubble. Recheck your numbers.

Go to the TV. Ninety percent of the time it will come up immediately. In any case, navigate the menus to the signal strength screens of the setup menu. Use satellite 110. You will either see colored strength bars or have the message 'not acquired'. Walkie-talkies are very handy at for the next step: Have a helper read off the 'not acquired' message or the signal strength number continuously as you swing the dish in tiny 3° increments, first right, then left until you acquire a signal. You will never have to adjust the skewing to acquire and you will seldom need to adjust the elevation. It you are using a plumb mast, you will always get a signal by carefully swinging left and right. When you have acquired, tighten the mast mount wing nuts.

After you acquire a signal, fine tune for maximum. Use a 7/16 inch socket on a ¼ inch drive ratchet wrench. First, loosen the elevation wing nuts slightly and use the wrench on the adjusting nut to carefully increase elevation, as your helper continues to announce numeric readings. Increase or decrease as necessary to get the largest number possible. Tight the elevation wing nuts and repeat the procedure on the heading adjustment fine tuning nut. You should obtain a numeric reading of over 90. You are finished.

I know this sounds complicated. After all, satellite repairmen get paid next to nothing to do this every day. They have a special instrument to help them acquire single-handedly at the dish. This instrument is well over $500, so I'll stick with using a helper. After a while you can do this whole thing in less than 15 minutes.

Flat Screen Mounting

I fondly remember the days of hauling around that gigantic 120 pound 4:3 35 inch picture tube TV set. You remember, that huge thing that used 300 watts and was constantly sliding around in its cabinet like a giant bowling ball.

The conversion to digital TV is now complete. The migration to 16:9 aspect ratio content has accelerated. Fewer and fewer programs are 4:3 aspect ratio. Many providers are switching to providing modern 16:9 material in letterbox format for 4:3 TV sets, greatly reducing the sharpness of the content to squeeze it onto an older screen format. The price of flat screens has never been lower.

The time to upgrade has arrived. But here we are with those custom oak trimmed cabinets we think are some kind of TV altar than cannot be defiled by us lowly TV viewers with a saw and a hammer. It's easier than you think.

It's true that most RV TV sets are too small by necessity. TV was an afterthought squeezed into an available cubby hole. But we didn't mind because we had to back away anyway to avoid seeing the lines and the snow. Digital television is different. We need to view the picture at a minimum distance to avoid seeing the dots, and at a maximum distance to avoid missing the detail. And now days a TV in the rig is considered a necessity.

For flat screen viewing, my rule of thumb is to take the advertised diagonal screen size in inches and divide by 10. The result gives the minimum viewing distance in feet. Multiply this number by 2 and you have the maximum viewing distance in feet. For example, a 32 inch flat screen should be viewed at least 3.2 feet away and no more than 6.4 feet away.

Next, we measure the distance from the TV to the seating area. This will define the screen size that is appropriate for that area. You will generally find that no matter what you do in an older RV, you will be too far away from the screen for the size you need, with no way to fit a larger screen into the space available.

There are many solutions: ceiling mounted tip down screens, pop up screens, and stored under the bed screens. But these are reserved for custom expensive high-end rigs. I will describe some of the less expensive ways to upgrade that space that came with your rig.

Older motor homes tend to have a space above the driver's seat in the overhead console dedicated for a TV and a shelf or cubby in the bedroom for another smaller set. In most cases we can mount a flat screen outside the hole using a swiveling adjustable wall mount. The mount is secured in the hole at right angles to the set. We want it mounted as close to the opening as we can. This allow us to pull the screen away from the opening to access the large vacated space behind the set, and swing it left or right of center. It also allows us to push it up against the opening to close off the hole for a "finished" look. We want a screen that will mask the entire vertical opening, and as a result it will overlap horizontally. We want it as wide as possible without interfering with adjacent cabinet doors. It is important to use a strong mount; RVs bump around and we want the screen secure from shaking when we are in motion.

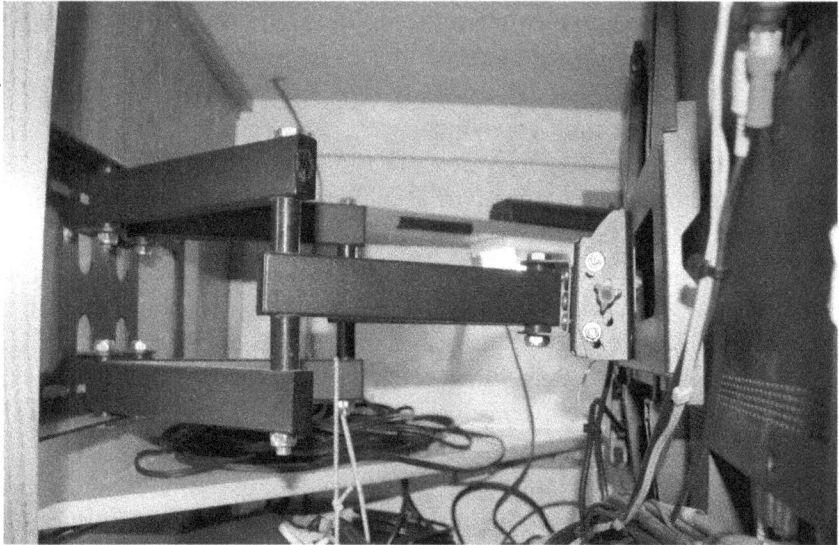

Above is a 40 inch screen on a heavy duty dual bar swivel mount. The side wall panel had to be reinforced with ½ inch plywood for rigidity and braced with two diagonal shelves. A small bungee cord loop supports the cabling. A small piece of stainless toilet flush valve chain secures the left side from sliding aft on the road. The right side is jammed into the cabinet corner stopping fore and aft movement.

The set can be adjusted 90° left and right to optimize the viewing angle. The cabinet had to be enlarged on top by removal of a faux oak spacer board. The oak crown moulding remains. A strip of black speaker cloth was stapled to the inside of the top of the cabinet space to hide the interior of the top of the cabinet, while allowing the set to be freely moved from its storage location in the cabinet to the viewing position. A small oak cabinet door was added on the right to allow access to the interior of the cabinet when the TV is out in its regular viewing position. (The slide out room is not extended as pictured.)

I have installed many smaller sets using this same mounting arrangement in other rigs. It's nice to be able to store the larger sets in the old TV cabinet while in motion. Smaller sets can be secured by using small cup hooks in the wood frame behind the set. A small 20 gauge wire is wrapped around the screws securing the set's rear cover at the top corners. This wire is twisted around the cup hooks. The wire can be quickly unhooked to allow movement of the set and access to the cabinet. These mounting arrangements are road tested.

One final note on flat screen TV selection. Stick with LED backlit sets commonly referred to as LED TVs. While LCD backlit sets seem to look better than LED sets, LCD sets use nearly twice as much electricity as do LED sets in the same screen size. This can be a deal breaker in an RV. LED sets are also thinner and lighter making them more suitable for our 'moveable picture frame' mounting techniques.

Getting On Line

As soon as the dish is set up and the TV is working, the next thing the kids want is internet access. After all, how are they going to share all their fun moments with their friends back home?

WIFI seems to be the method of choice. It is available at most RV parks in some form and usually can be bootlegged from your friends or relatives when you are visiting. While 3G and 4G phones are even more ubiquitous, they are an expensive and low bandwidth approach that I only use in a pinch.

Most WIFI systems that are available are secured systems for which you must pay, usually on a per device basis. This can make using anything more than one laptop device get expensive quickly.

Many years ago I was visiting an RV park/casino on Boulder Hiway in Las Vegas. I was attending a convention of fellow Dodge Ram owners, and we had a package deal on the space rent. I arrived early and was looking forward to setting up my new rig and reporting back to my friends on the status quo; many of them were arriving later that day.

I hooked up to the RV park's telephone system, using my rig external phone jack plugged in to the park's RV phone jack service. Wow! That was easy! I had dial tone and only had to dial 9 to get an outside line. I quickly set up my laptop's modem to dial 9, and dial my ISP's local Las Vegas phone number. Presto! I had dial-up internet service and started emailing everyone. When I went to check out I had an extra $100 worth of telephone usage charges! The lousy RV park was charging me by the minute even on local calls!

Time to find another way to get on line...

My how times have changed. That external telephone jack on my RV hasn't seen any use since that Vegas trip. Cell phones killed the telephone star. WIFI killed everyone else. So how do we use that single WIFI laptop connection to provide our every need? We use our own router, isolated on its own subnet.

This all presupposes that we can connect to the WIFI from our rig. Many parks have hot spots scattered all around and some require you to go to the office to gain access. More and more, park owner laziness is taking over and the WIFI job is being farmed out, or at least, hot spots are appearing all over the park.

To reliably access these hot spots from your rig, you will usually need more than the WIFI antenna and transceiver in your laptop. I use an Alfa AWUS036H 1 watt transceiver mounted in my refrigerator vent. It also has a 9 db gain antenna attached.

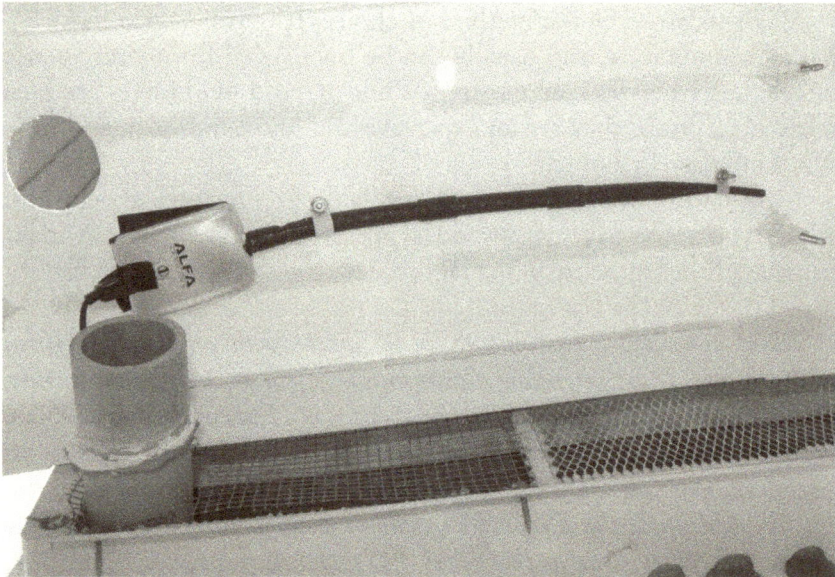

I use black tape to weather-proof the antenna and USB connectors. The Alfa is attached with Velcro to the inside of the vent and the antenna is screwed onto the underside with nylon wire clamps and 6-32 stainless steel screws. The USB cable is routed to the laptop. USB cables can be no longer than 15 feet without a hub or repeater. The Alfa is a 1000mw transceiver and can draw close to the 500ma limit allowable to a USB device. It is important that you connect this directly to your laptop or use a powered USB hub. I burned up the motherboard 5 volt power supply in a small Toshiba B142 I was using for the Alfa, so make sure you power the Alfa USB externally especially if you need to run a powered USB extension to get all the way from the refer vent to your laptop.

The Alfa software is Windows XP/ Windows 7 compatible. You will need a laptop that has a wired NIC (a plug for a wired internet connection) and at least two USB 2.0 ports. You will also need an inexpensive wireless router (preferably one that runs on 12 volts!) and a network cable to connect them together. Since this laptop will need to be running all the time, find a way to power it from your rig 12 volt battery. That way an AC power interruption will not take your network down.

First, plug the Alfa into a USB port. Remember which port you use because the software needs to be reinstalled if you later use a different port. Install the software and search for available networks. Signal strength numbers greater than 80 are best. You should be able to find your park's WIFI service as a connection choice. Connect to it. Follow the park's directions on your browser and establish an internet connection. Verify you can browse to a web page of your choice. You may need to delete your browser temporary internet files to make sure you are accessing a live web page and not a cached copy.

After you have established internet access on your laptop set up your laptop for Internet Connection Sharing (ICS) as follows:

Using Windows XP, Start, Settings, Control Panel. Start Network Connections. Right click on the connection for the Realtek Alfa. Click on Properties. Click on the Advanced tab. Click on the ICS Allow box. In settings, add every available service to the list of shared services (unless you are an IT guy and want to pick and choose.)

Now right click on the Local Area Connection (that supports the laptop's wired NIC). Click on Properties. Scroll down and click on Internet Protocol (TCP/IP). Click on Properties. Click on Alternate Configuration. Click on User Configured. Enter 192.168.0.1 into the IP address boxes. Enter 255.255.255.0 into the Subnet mask boxes. You have finished ICS setup. Don't worry, this only has to be done the first time! When you reboot it will all come up fine.

Now power up your wireless router. Plug a network cord between your laptop shared wired NIC port and the router WLAN port. The WLAN port is the one that is not grouped with the other wired ports on the router and it is usually labeled.

Using a second laptop, connect to the wireless router, either wirelessly or via a second network cable between your second laptop and any router LAN port. Set up the router using the manufacturer's documentation. I recommend using a wired connection to configure the router initially.

You will now have your own router in your rig that uses the first laptop and the Alfa as a wireless uplink. You will need to keep the first laptop running and accessible because some parks (like KOA) want you to log in again every day. It is also convenient to check on the uplink quality periodically, especially if your uplink is of marginal signal strength.

If you have a MagicJack this can be plugged into the second USB port of laptop one. If you have MagicJack Plus, it can plug into the router. The MagicJack can then be jacked into the rig telephone system, and you will have normal dial tone throughout the rig. Or you can plug a cordless telephone base set into the MagicJack. I recommend a DECT 6.0 based cordless phone system to avoid interference with the WIFI system.

To top it off, you can connect your streaming equipped Blu Ray players and XBOX 360 consoles directly into your router and enjoy XBOX Live or Netflix streaming through the same uplink. You may have to disable the firewall and security features on laptop one to allow XBOX Live to play. Naturally, all the Ipods, Ipads, Nintendos, and other WIFI hobos work fine using the wireless router.

I have not tested this setup with Windows 7 or 8 but I understand both of the OS's support ICS. I have used this setup successfully at many campgrounds and at many friend's homes.

My router is stuck away under the kitchen cabinets along with a laptop DC to DC power supply and the connected MagicJack. These devices share a common 12 volt fuse position in the DC fuse panel, so they can be depowered as a group when I am dry camping and no uplink is available or desired.

I also carry a dedicated older laptop to serve as laptop one. It doesn't take much processing power to handle ICS duties; any old thing will do that can run Windows XP. If you're a real fossil you can even make ICS work on Windows 98 but I can't remember how!

The Fireplace Heater

We had a cold snap so I decided to install one of those cute fireplace heaters in the rig. I had been fretting for months deciding where to put it. It just didn't seem correct to have it under the TV set; there wasn't enough room anyway.

Under the counter? You would bang your legs on it and maybe get burned to boot. Most or these heaters were at least 30 inches wide and they all wanted to be wall mounted, at least 24 inches above the floor. Something had to be wrong with this requirement because I had seen these heaters in RV's mounted at floor level and in real stupid places like under cabinets. Who wants to enjoy their fireplace with dancing flames with a beautiful backdrop of faux oak?

Besides the esoteric stuff was the problem of power. These things need a fifteen amp AC circuit and can draw 1200 watts (10 amps) at full heat. I didn't want to look at the power cord. So it had to go somewhere where I could install an EXT PLUG. After all in the summer time I might want to have it running just to see the crackling flame effect at night while running the inverter. Or maybe I might really need it for heating. Its power source had to be both flexible and invisible.

Finally I had the idea. Why not mount it under the rear picture window? That way we could look out the window at nature with a crackling fake fire right under the view. Perfect at night.

The wall underneath the window had an outlet so I was confident I could pull in a new cord for an EXT PLUG. And not only that, the heater was in a practical location under a large window at the extreme rear of the rig, a poorly heated location since all the heat rose and moved forward along the upward sloping ceiling.

And so I ordered a nice cheap Electric Fireplace Heater (Estate Design Arlington WMAR) for $110 from Home Depot. It had a remote control, two heat levels, and a nice looking fake fire that could be operated with the actual heat turned off. It was only 24 inches wide and fit nicely under the window, with ½ inch to spare underneath. It had curved glass on the front so it only protruded 4 inches from the wall at its sides. This allows the recliners to store in their normal locations behind the slide outs, with room to spare for movement while in transit. It runs cool underneath. The curved glass also disguised the newly installed combination quad outlet containing the EXT PLUG circuit as well as a regular living room circuit. This completely hid the cord while allowing me to plug into either of two sources. The hanging bracket mounted nicely on the window frame.

I fired it up. It blew hot air upward from the top and away from the window. Perfect. The area around the base remains cold even after extensive operation, so the tight bottom clearance is not an issue. The fake fire effect is very good looking and has multiple levels of brightness. The fake coals are made of glass pieces. I glued them in place with epoxy so they won't shift and fall out on the road.

That Noisy Vent Fan

For my entire RVing career I have never figured out why we put up with that horrible Ventline fan. It is loud and sucks all of that expensive air conditioned air out of your rig whenever it's on.

I decided to make it two-speed. This is a simple modification to make. You will need a sheet metal chassis nibbler (available at Radio Shack for about $10) to make the square hole for the HI LO switch. The switch matches the Ventline ON OFF and light ON OFF switches. All the wiring is done in the corner circuit box behind the switches and can be done without removing the vent hood from the rig. The hole is .508 inches wide by .756 tall (½ x ¾ inches). Start off by drilling a 3/8 diameter hole with a drill in the mounting location.

Then use the nibbling tool to make the hole square. Be careful not to deface the plastic label as you go. The resistor is mounted anywhere convenient inside the box. Solder wires onto the switch and onto the resistor before mounting. The switch hole is a snug fit to secure the switch in place. You will need a small file to smooth out the hole edges, but be careful not to make the hole too large. Then complete the wiring, see schematic. Use wire nuts to make it easier.

Fan Wiring Modification "HI LO"

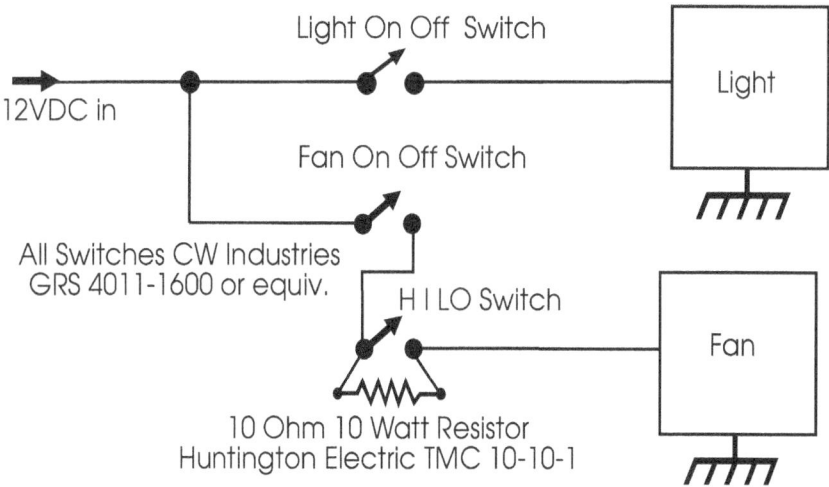

Light On Off Switch

12VDC in

Light

Fan On Off Switch

All Switches CW Industries
GRS 4011-1600 or equiv.

H I LO Switch

Fan

10 Ohm 10 Watt Resistor
Huntington Electric TMC 10-10-1

I always prop the outside vent door open with a one inch stick so the fan does not have to blow the vent open. This allows for quieter fan operation and more efficient air flow on low speed.

Three Way Bedroom Lights

It was a long reach for us, particularly with the bedroom slide in, to reach the bedroom ceiling light switch. Fortunately I had a matching fixture from a previous lighting change elsewhere in the rig. Each fixture had SPDT switches. If your fixtures have SPST switches (as used in the vent fan upgrade above) you will need to get SPDT switches for this modification (CW Industries GRS 4012-1600). I was able to fish the wiring through the overhead by removing the vent fan bezel. This gave access to the ceiling joist 2x4's which I could drill holes through for access to the space above the fixtures. The wiring is completed as shown in the schematic diagram below.

Three Way Light Switch

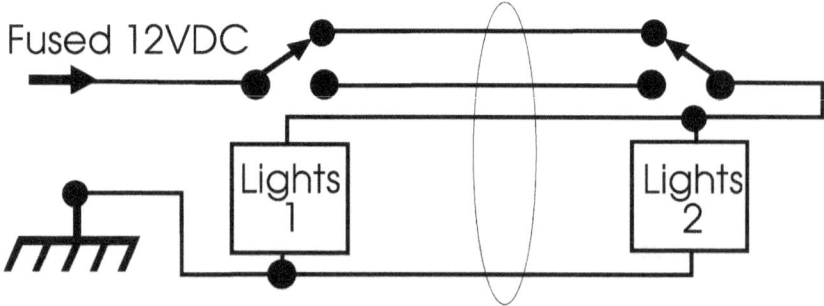

Fused 12VDC

Lights 1

Lights 2

Chapter 6

Transfer Switching Revisited

I have installed many inverter/transfer systems since my first book was published. I still use the same techniques and transfer arrangements for larger 3000 watt systems. But I have developed a newer way of transferring loads in smaller travel trailers and smaller Class 'C' motor homes. The main reason I have changed my methods in the smaller systems is to reduce the expense and to provide added flexibility.

In many rigs there is just not enough space for more than two batteries, and no demand for more electricity than it takes to run a microwave oven and a small flat screen. These rigs are candidates for smaller 1800 to 2000 watt inverters such as the Samlex 2000-12. I try to avoid brands other than Samlex and Xantrex. I have had trouble with other brands failing prematurely. Other brands also seem to use proprietary battery connection posts, sometimes requiring extra cabling as well as internal modifications to disconnect the built in ground fault. Also, these two brands have user-friendly warranty and return policies, and well designed remote control features.

The need for short cabling and secure connections is just as important small or large. Compact installations are actually more difficult because of limited mounting space. They take considerable preplanning and are more labor intensive than large rig installations.

The new transfer switching scheme is somewhat simplified. Each transfer relay is pre-wired outside of the rig. The MJN relays used are about the size of a giant ice cube and enclosed in a plastic case. I use #14 black stranded wires for the 3 hot pigtails and #14 white stranded wire for the neutral pigtails. I also label the pairs so that it is easy to identify them during installation in the box. Make the pigtails about twelve inches long. Use #20 solid jumper wire to connect the relay coil to the off-normal contact set. See drawing below.

Simplified Transfer Relay, Single Circuit

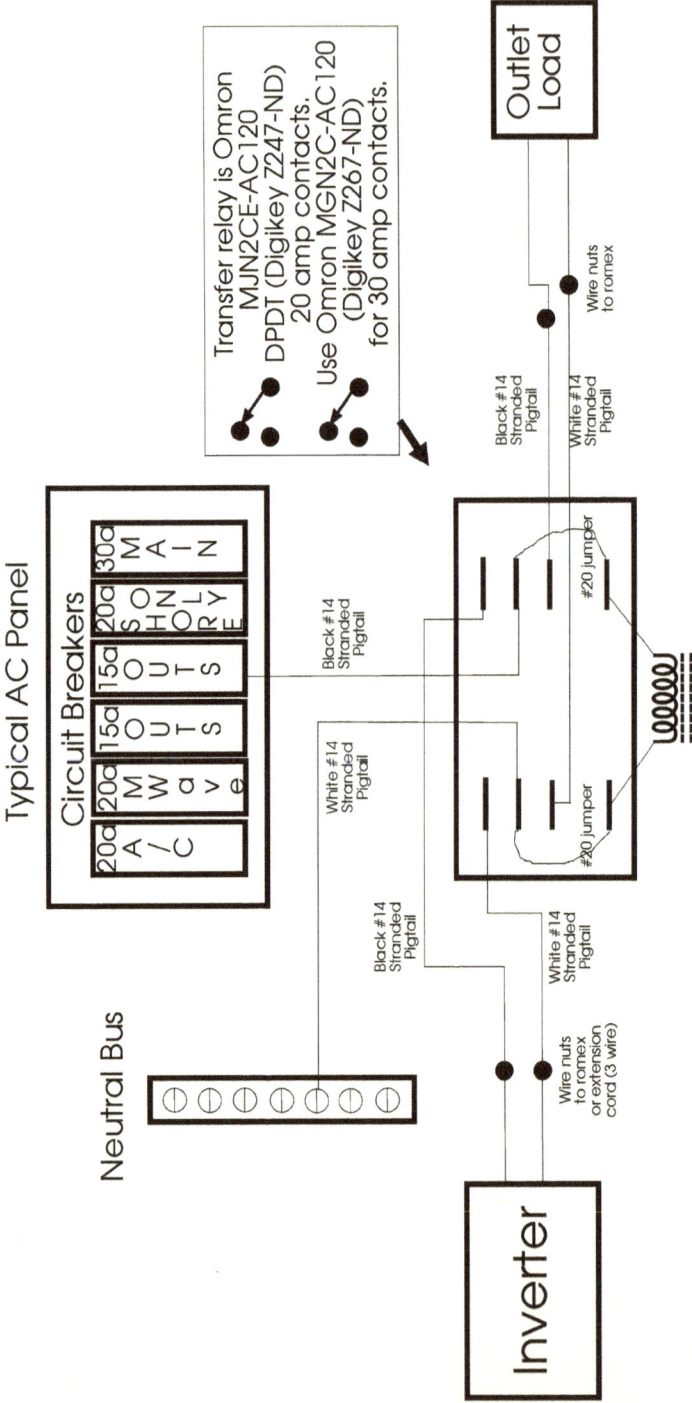

Typical AC Panel

Circuit Breakers

20a	20a	15a	20a	30a
A / C	M W a v e	S O U T S	S H U T O F F S	M A I N

Neutral Bus

Transfer relay is Omron MJN2CE-AC120 DPDT (Digikey Z247-ND) 20 amp contacts. Use Omron MGN2C-AC120 (Digikey Z267-ND) for 30 amp contacts.

Black #14 Stranded Pigtail

White #14 Stranded Pigtail

Black #14 Stranded Pigtail

White #14 Stranded Pigtail

Wire nuts to romex or extension cord (3 wire)

Inverter

Outlet Load

Wire nuts to romex

Black #14 Stranded Pigtail

White #14 Stranded Pigtail

#20 jumper

#20 jumper

Relay Viewed from Bottom

Only one relay is shown in the above circuit for clarity. Three of these circuits will usually fit in the space beneath the circuit breakers. If not, they can be placed in the space behind the panel. Wrap these relays in black plastic electrician's tape, paying special attention to wrap the bottom area where the exposed contacts are located.

Since they are wrapped in tape, it is important to identify the contact pairs while you can still see them with labels. Label them "Inverter," "Line," and "Load."

The circuit is designed so that the relays close whenever shore power is present to the circuit breaker from the shore power feed. This is completely the reverse of how most inverter transfer relays operate. Basically we are transferring the loads from the inverter to shore power whenever shore power is present. These relays have a minimal current draw of about 60ma, but we can better spare those 5 watts (per relay) when on shore power than when on batteries. After all 15 watts translates into about one amp of battery draw that we don't need! And we won't miss the 15 watts at all when plugged in to shore power.

In its simplest form, we usually use three relays to transfer three circuits: The microwave and two outlet circuits. The remaining circuits are never transferred: the air conditioner, and the 'shore only.' I generally rewire the panel to group the 'shore only' circuits together onto a single breaker, or onto two shore only breakers if space is available in the panel for additional breakers. The 'shore only' loads are: the refrigerator, the converter, and the electric water heater (if equipped,) and obviously the air conditioner.

The air conditioner needs to be on its own 20 amp circuit since it draws about 14 amps continuously. The refrigerator draws about 4 amps. The converter uses from 2 to 9 amps depending on the load. An electric water heater draws about 11 amps. So we are constrained to find enough 'shore only' breaker capacity to satisfy these loads.

It is also usually necessary to install an additional outlet for the refrigerator to use. Normally the refrigerator is plugged into an outlet circuit that we want to invert, and we don't want to use the inverter to supply the energy for the refrigerator. Much better to use propane. The refrigerator can be forced to gas operation, but most dry campers forget to do this and run their battery down the first night by accident! So take the extra effort up front and run a new outlet in, bringing the romex into the shore power panel, where it is tied down with another 'shore only' load like the converter.

The relay installation is simple. Just remove the romex load black wire from its circuit breaker and remove its corresponding white wire from the neutral bus. Use wire nuts to connect these wires to the "load" pigtails from the transfer relay. Then connect the "line" wires from the relay back to the breaker and the neutral bus. Finally, wire nut the "inverter" pigtails to the cord that runs to the inverter power plug. One circuit done; repeat for the others. All the "inverter" wires can be combined and 'wire nutted' to a single inverter cord. I usually use a #12 three wire extension cord. The male end is plugged in to the inverter. The cord is routed to the shore power panel, where the female end is cut off. The cord end is then routed into the box.

Usually all three relays can be stuffed into the bottom of the box under the breakers. This makes for a very compact and safe arrangement. In very tight circumstances the pigtails may need to be shortened to eliminate excess wire in the box. Just make sure not to mix up your 'load', 'line', and 'inverter' relay wires.

Additional Benefits

Using this transfer scheme has some advantages that were unforeseen when I dreamed it up. We already discussed the power saving when dry camping. The inverter is not called upon to power the transfer relays, so we save a continuous 1 amp battery load while inverting at dry camp.

Since the neutrals are isolated between the inverter and the shore power feed by virtue of our transfer relay wiring, we can do some neat tricks with the shore power circuit breakers.

Let's say we have a low current GFI circuit available for our use, but it is insufficient to run our rig microwave and TV set. Just like the "Less than 30 amps Available" scenario of Chapter 4.

We can flip off the shore panel circuit breakers that would normally power our transfer relays e.g. the microwave, outlet one, and outlet two breakers. This allows these circuits to fall back to inverter power, with its isolated neutral. We turn on the inverter and are able to power these circuits *while using the GFIC connected to the shore cord feed to simultaneously charge the battery via the converter on its 'shore only' circuit.* That allows our meager shore circuit to keep our batteries charged while we use the inverter for those higher current demands. Of course we would never want to use the air conditioner, nor the electric water heater, which would overload the shore supply.

We might, however, tinker with using the electric refrigerator option....!

Another unsuspected benefit arises for those with a small generator. It may be used in the same way, charging your battery (and maybe even running your air conditioner if it's a Honda EU3000) while you use the inverter for your demand current loads. I have found both of these scenarios to work perfectly with this most simple transfer system.

You may wonder if your going to blow up your inverter doing all this trick stuff. I blew up two inverters in my early tinkering with transfer switching. In both cases it was caused by back feeding shore power into the inverter. So this is a very valid question.

In the beginning I used transfer relays that were powered from the inverter. When the inverter was powered down, the relays would revert back to shore power. This method is used most predominantly today. Commercial transfer relays for inverter and generator use, like Progressive Dynamics PD52V ($240,) use a single large DPDT relay, which is time delayed on make. The relay switches both the hot lead and the neutral lead and is designed to transfer all loads in the house to the inverter (or generator) after a few second startup delay. When the inverter shuts down, the relay releases.

Unfortunately inverters don't shut off cleanly. They sort of fade away when they shut down. If they have a large load on them, they will shut off quickly. If they have little load on them, they take nearly two seconds to fade down to zero volts output. If you are powering transfer relays with an inverter some interesting things happen when you shut the inverter down.

As the voltage fades down the relay magnetic energy gets weaker until the relay begins to chatter. It doesn't break cleanly, it vibrates a couple of times until it breaks. This effect is most apparent on modified sine wave inverters, but it happens on sinusoidal inverters as well. If you are using a single relay contact on a single switched load, the 'chatter won't matter,' because the load will either be on the shore side or the inverter side at any instant, never both at once. It therefore does not matter if the shore power side is energized; the relay can never be in both states simultaneously and the inverter can never see the shore power present on that normally closed contact.

On the other hand, if you are using two or more relay contacts to switch the same load (as I did in my first book's transfer system), it is a certainty that one relay will chatter at a different rate than the other relay. This is fatal for an inverter since the inverter output will be momentarily crossed with shore power during shutdown.

So, can that happen with our simplified three relay system described above? No. For two reasons. First, the relays are powered by clean commercial power. When it is switched off, it's off. No chatter. Not even with inverter generators. When they shut off, it's instant.

Second, each relay is dedicated to one load. Only one contact is involved on the hot lead and the neutral is also switched. So not only is it impossible to cross the inverter with shore power, it's impossible to cross the neutrals. So we can flip those breakers on and off with impunity no matter whether shore power is present, and no matter whether the inverter is on or off, and never hurt anything.

So this simplified system achieves the benefits of simultaneous charging and load balancing in a safe and inexpensive way. It is true that there are no individual circuit breakers on the inverted circuits. But small inverters cannot deliver enough current to overload these circuits to the point of overheat. They also are equipped with a 20 amp master breaker. Many models are also GFI protected, which will work just fine with our isolated neutral setup. The inverter can't even see that old culprit, the park supplied ground fault!

One final tip: Always mount your inverter on a wooden wall or floor. Many small inverters internally bond the neutral to the metal chassis of the inverter. They also connect the green ground wire to the metal chassis. They want to pretend that they are a commercial utility.

This bonding creates a ground fault that will back-feed into your rig. If your inverter has such bonding, do not connect the green ground wire on your feed extension cord to the rig ground bus. Since the inverter battery supply leads are usually isolated from the inverter chassis ground and your inverter is not screwed into a grounded metal part on your rig, no ground fault is created.

If you must mount the inverter onto a metal grounded part of the rig, it is usually possible to disassemble the inverter partially to expose the neutral and remove the connection to ground. Most higher end inverters are designed to allow this type of modification. You may also want to remove any GFI outlet on the inverter and replace it with a conventional outlet.

Chapter 7

Outside the Rig

The big trend now days is to buy a pair of Honda 2000 generators and connect them for a total of 4000 watts. The availability of dual feed gas tanks like the BERGS system make the run times nearly 24 hours at full capacity. Two-thousands really need an external fuel tank; they run dry in about 4 hours at full load.

To bridge Honda 2000's, it is not necessary to buy the custom interconnect cable. It is only necessary to plug one generator into the other using a short double male extension cord.

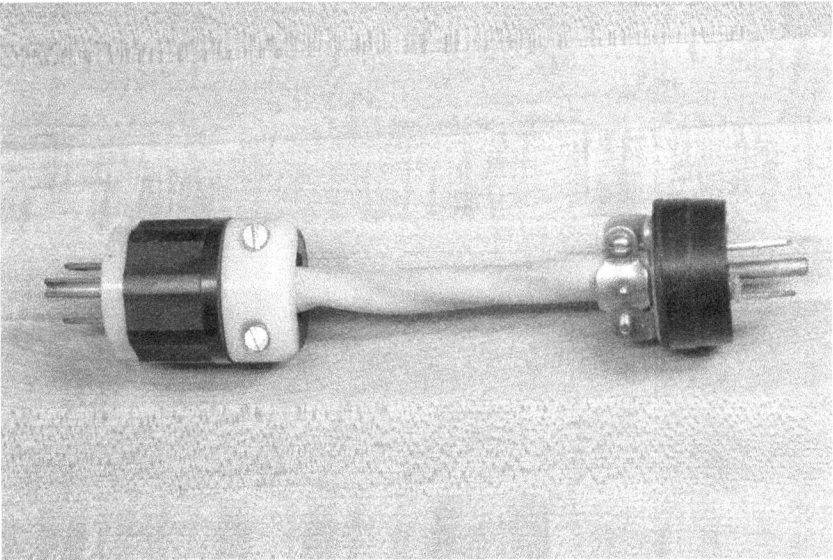

The one pictured above is really too short to use, but you get the idea. Make sure to get black to black and white to white on the plugs. You will cause trouble if you reverse the wires. Also be careful! If one end is plugged into power, the other male end is energized and will be a shock hazard. Plug in both ends before starting either generator.

It does not matter which receptacle on each generator you plug the connector in to. They are wired in common inside, and also commonly wired to the proprietary connectors for the proprietary interconnect cable. Any unused receptacle can be used to power the load.

Since I own a EU3000is and a EU2000, I naturally tried to parallel them, hoping to get 5000 watts. It does work. Unfortunately the 2000 takes the brunt of the load while the 3000 idles along. Thus you really cannot obtain 5000 watts. At about 3500 watts the Honda 2000 overloads and trips off line. I guess that is why Honda does not recommend bridging generators of dissimilar size.

I prefer the EU3000is over even a single 2000 because it is noticeably quieter, particularly so when the economy mode is used. The 3000 has a better noise rating and an 8 hour run capacity between fill-ups at full load with its 3 gallon tank. As I have pointed out earlier, the use of a single small generator in conjunction with an inverter is more efficient and quieter than constantly running a generator that will carry the full rig load. And you can shut the generator down in the evening without losing power (except to the air conditioner.)

Outside Outlets

It seems when you have power all the time, you find more ways to use it. Even outside the rig. My slide out rooms had 120 VAC power wired to them through a flexible coiled extension cord. The cord was terminated on a box on the frame at one end and a box on the slide out at the other end. They were standard electrical boxes; they had cover plates, which could easily be removed. The box on the slide out side was easily accessible with the slide out extended so why not install an exterior duplex outlet? Done!

Refer Fan

I work on a lot of RV refrigerators. When refrigerators are installed in slide out rooms, the top vent cannot be mounted on the roof of the slide out; an additional access fixture vent is mounted above the normal servicing opening to allow the hot air flowing up the back of the refrigerator to escape. Smaller refrigerators such as those mounted in cab-over campers come from the factory with a small fan on the condenser fins at the top of the refer backside.

Dometic and Norcold are economy minded and never provide any more evaporative cooling capacity than they need to. Keeping the coils and condenser cooled is essential to efficient operation of gas absorption refrigerators. That is why RV manufacturers add a baffle in the rear of the refrigerator space to force the convected cooling air over the coils and the condenser.

I had noticed that my refrigerator inside temperature was warmer when the weather outside was hot, particularly so when outside temperatures exceeded 100°F. In fact, Dometic supplies a relay accessory that provides a closed circuit to operate a fan whenever the refrigerator is turned on. Why would they do that? I had seen this relay factory installed in slide out mounted refers. It must be to improve the rear air flow. The tiny little computer style fan they used was mounted on the condenser. It had a small thermal switch, which was pop-riveted to the condenser fins.

I was sure I could improve on that. I found a 12 volt "O2" fan at Walmart for about $10. It even came with a power cord. So now all I had to do was find a way to automatically turn it on when it got too hot outside. An attic fan switch! I went to a local appliance parts house for mine but Grainger sells a comparable unit for $23 (Air Vent Model 58070). This switch can be set to close at any temperature between 50 and 120°F. The fan is just wired through the switch to the refrigerator 12 volt supply. So the fan switches on automatically whenever the outside temperature exceeds your set point. I have mine set to 100°F. It noticeably improves the refrigerator cooling efficiency in hot weather. The fan is secured with round head wood screws that extend out of the wood base. The O2 fan has notched mounting holes. The fan can be slid off the screws and removed from the cavity when refer maintenance is required. I used 10 feet of #20 two conductor wire for the fan power cord so that the fan does not have to be disconnected when removed.

You will also notice the Belkin USB powered repeater for the Alfa WIFI transceiver on the right of the picture. You also may have noticed the piece of two inch PVC on the right. It is stepped on a wooden plug on the refer mounting box floor. The pipe extends upward and out of the roof mounted refrigerator vent (see the Alfa mounting picture.) It is normally capped with a PVC cap.

This rooftop cap can be removed and a 25 foot telescoping fiberglass pole is inserted into the pipe, providing a handy flag pole. This pole serves double duty as a support for a vertical wire antenna. This wire is connected to my ham radio screwdriver antenna, effectively making a center loaded 160M vertical about 40 feet high. And you can have a big windsock to boot!

Back Up Lights

I was working on adding an emergency extra outlet in a small travel trailer so that Joe could use his electric heater without tripping his overloaded bathroom GFI. It was an early winter evening and dusk had already set in. Suddenly there was the sound of crunching fiberglass. Joe and I ran outside. A large fifth wheel was backing into the space next to Joe's. The Alpenlite fifth wheel had been backed into the electric riser and crushed the left lower corner of the rear bonnet. The driver was looking on intently; he said he had just bought the rig and was still learning how to maneuver it...

Time after time we hear stories of expensive backing crashes. Some people just resort to pull-through sites or daytime only parking. Others keep their neighbors awake by arriving at night with flashlights and shouting as they back between trees, rocks, and other booby traps that park owners and the Forest Service have placed in perfect spots to damage your rig.

While there is no stopping the placement of these obstacles, at least we can be aware of their presence with proper lighting as we back into our site. Most rigs have only the most mediocre back-up lighting. A system like the one below can be installed onto the back of any vehicle: trailer, truck, or motor home.

The light assemblies are Par 36 Rubber Tractor/Utility Lamps, available from Napa, Grainger, and others for about $14 each. The 36 watt sealed beam bulbs have screw terminals. The rubber housings protect the bulbs and don't corrode or discolor. The sealed beam bulbs are long lasting and reliable in the dirty area near the ground, where it can get wet and rocks can fly. The lamps mount with a single bolt, which allows for rotation and tilt to any angle. They are also very bright.

Since these bulbs draw about 3 amps each, they usually will overload the vehicle backup light circuit (if one exists) and therefore a 40 amp automotive relay is used to supply them from the vehicle or coach battery. The relay is operated whenever the vehicle back up light circuit is energized. See schematic diagram.

Back Up Light Relay

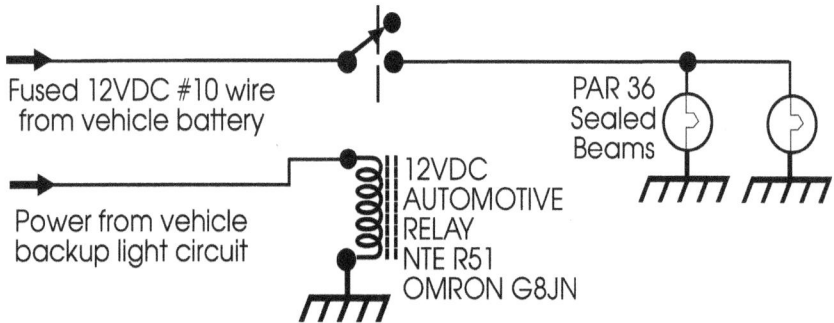

Fused 12VDC #10 wire
from vehicle battery

PAR 36
Sealed
Beams

Power from vehicle
backup light circuit

12VDC
AUTOMOTIVE
RELAY
NTE R51
OMRON G8JN

If you are installing this setup on a truck or motor home you will need to tap onto the wire that goes to the backup light bulbs. If you have a seven conductor trailer plug for towing, this wire will be found on the center pin of the plug, the round one in the middle. This wire is connected to the relay coil, as shown above.

If you are installing this on the rear of a trailer or fifth wheel, the installation will depend on whether the trailer already has back up lights installed. If it does, tap in to the backup light bulb wiring in the rear for relay coil power. You will need to run a large #10 or #12 wire to the fuse panel to supply the bulbs. Use a 15 amp fuse.

If you have no existing back up lights, trace the seven-way trailer towing cable to its connection box. The wire to the seven-way center pin is yellow. Whenever the towing vehicle is in reverse, 12 volts should be present on this wire. It is designed to provide about 2 amps only so we need to connect this wire to the relay.

Mount the relay forward, near (or inside) the connector box. 12 volts to run the lamps can be obtained from the large black wire and ground from the large white wire. Use a 15 amp fuse and run a #10 wire from the relay to the rear of the rig for the lamps.

You may want to add a switch where you can close the relay manually. See the picture below. Just put the switch from the fused #10 to the relay coil wire. This allows you to manually switch on the backup lamps, even when not in reverse. The seven-way cord doesn't even have to be connected to the towing vehicle for this switch to work. The lamps run off of the coach battery. The use of #10 or #12 wiring to the lamps makes sure the voltage to the lamps is maximized for brightest light.

Replacement PAR 36 sealed beam lamps are available at most auto parts stores. Make sure they have the same connection terminals. Some replacements are not furnished with screwdriver terminals. Replacements easily snap in to the rubber housings.

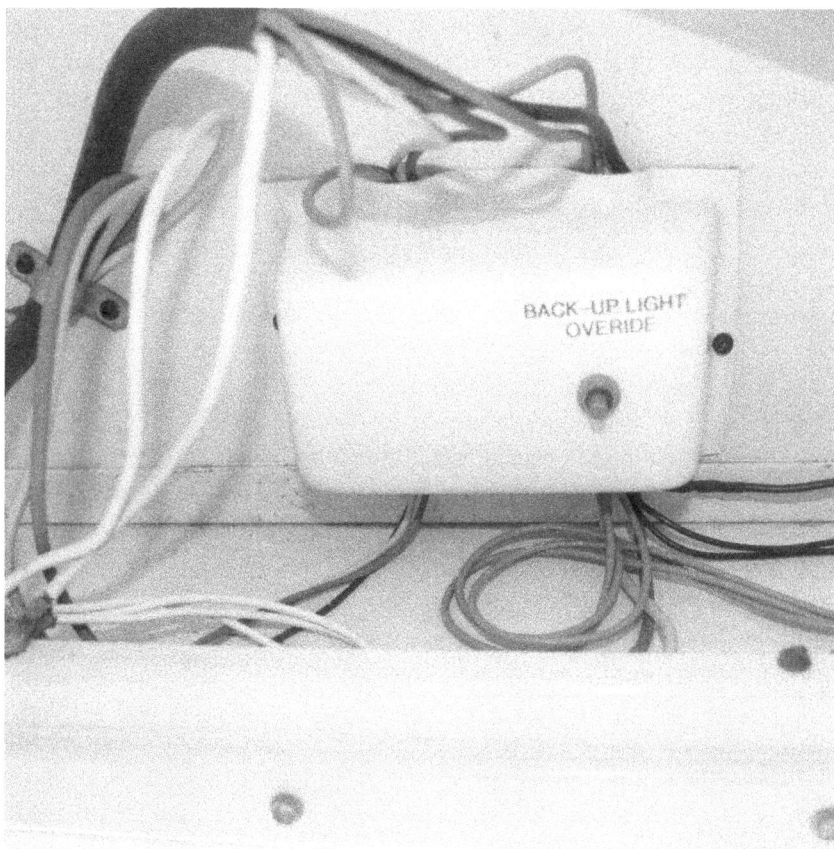

Refrigerators

The most common things I repair on RV's are the appliances. Since the most expensive appliance on most RV's is the refrigerator, you should service it regularly and always level your rig.

Let me briefly explain how these critters work. They use a process called gas absorption using ammonia as the gas. The ammonia gas has a small amount of rust inhibitor mixed in to keep the inside of all those tubes from corroding. The energy source for a gas absorption refer is a small amount of heat which is supplied from either an electric element or a small gas flame.

The heat makes the ammonia vaporize and rise to the top of the refer. As it falls down through the tubes by gravity, it condenses back into a liquid and absorbs heat in the process. When it gets to the bottom it is reheated again.

It is absolutely essential that the refer be set up vertically so that the ammonia will fall by gravity through the large helical tubes on the back of the refer. If you remove the access cover you will see the helical tubes (along with the burner assembly in the bottom right corner.) You can use a torpedo level on those tubes. Any tube that is level and not going downhill will stop the refer from cooling.

Now you see why you must keep your rig level. It is not so important side to side, but very important front to rear if your refer is mounted on either side of your rig. If the refer is mounted against the rear wall, side to side level becomes more important than front to rear. Just observe with the torpedo level if you are not sure; those tubes MUST allow liquid ammonia to flow downhill.

The bad news is if you operate the refer when it is not flowing downhill, the rust inhibitor in the ammonia will crystallize from excessive heat. The small crystals that are formed will block some of the tiny orifices in the ammonia system. *This irreversible damage can only be repaired by replacing the entire cooling unit system.* Cooling units are very expensive; replacement cost plus labor is very close to the price of a new refrigerator. It only takes a 10° slope to cause trouble, so be very careful. I see the most defective cooling units on horse trailers with living units. Get some horse sense!

The source of power for a gas refer is a small amount of heat. That heat is provided by one of three methods: propane flame, 120 VAC heating element, or 12 VDC heating element. If your refer is a 'three way' unit, it can use any of these methods. More common are 'two way' units which use either propane or 120 VAC house current. Now days, three way units are usually found only in small refers installed in cab-over campers and pop-up tent trailers. Nearly all units installed in larger rigs are two way.

Two way units are equipped with a small electronics board which controls the refer operation. This board requires 12 volts DC to operate. The 12 volt coach battery must be charged for this board to work. The board uses very little electricity (less than 1 amp) but it must have over 11 volts of battery to operate properly. The battery is not used to actually create the heat for the ammonia in two way models, only to run the electronics. In three way models, the battery is also called upon to heat the ammonia in the 'DC' mode. The DC heat element draws over 30 amps from the battery.

Common two way models can be forced to use propane (GAS mode) or left to automatically choose (AUTO mode). When left on AUTO, the control board detects if 120 VAC current is available at the refer plug. If so, if uses an AC heat element (which looks just like a DC heat element) to create the heat to power the cooling process. If 120 VAC current is not available, the control board decides to use gas, and starts the process to ignite the propane flame.

In gas operation, the control board opens the electrically controlled gas valve and signals the reigniter module to begin sparking to ignite the gas. As soon as the flame ignites, the reigniter detects flame and stops sparking. Within 15 seconds the flame will heat the thermocouple detector sufficiently to signal the control board that the flame is on.

If the flame fails to ignite, the control board will wait a few seconds are try again. After three failed attempts, the 'CHECK' light will come on. The most common trouble when you see a 'CHECK' light is that you have run out of propane.

The control board senses the temperature inside the refer box with a small thermocouple. Inside the box, you will see a small white wire emerging from the back of the refer, which goes up to a sliding white plastic thermocouple holder. The thermocouple itself is about the size of a bee-bee and is inside the holder. The holder is attached to the metal fins of the cooling evaporator and can be slid up for lower box temperature and down for higher temperature. This is your thermostat on these basic models. When the control unit detects that the box is cool enough, it shuts off the heat source to the ammonia system.

As you can see, the ammonia system is the cooling workhorse here and it doesn't really care where the heat comes from for it to work. The 120 VAC heating element (pictured below) uses between 325 and 450 watts (3½ to 5 amps) in operation. Refer propane consumption is very low. Many people see the small flame and presume it is only a pilot light! The burner tube is pictured below.

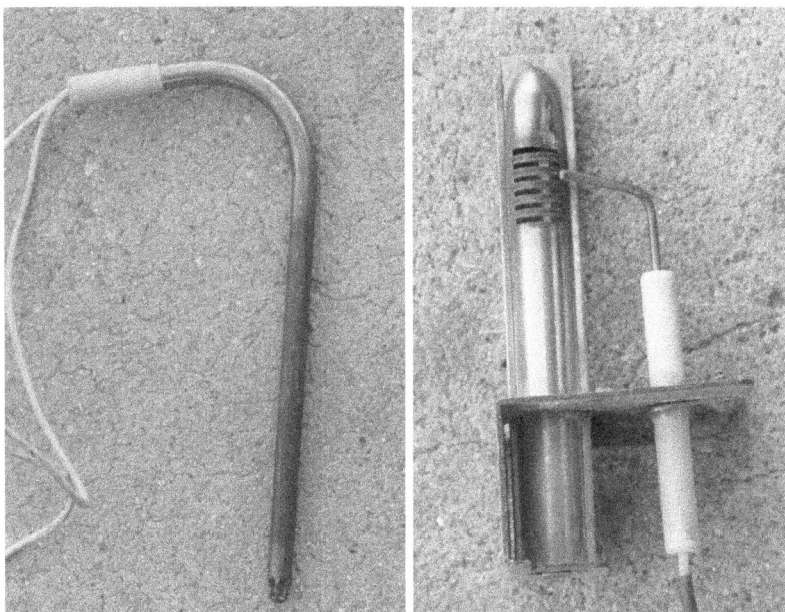

The AC (and DC when equipped) heat elements are replaceable and located inside a sheet metal door on the side of the up pipe above the propane heating assembly. Make sure to use the correct wattage unit for your specific model; 325 watt (part number 17 37 68-03/7) is the most common on Dometic two way models.

The propane heat burner tube will fill with rust particles and will need to be removed and cleaned or blown out with compressed air annually. When dirty, the flame will be orange instead of blue.

The most common replacement part I use on Dometic refrigerators is the spark ignition device, the reigniter. They either will not spark at all or will not stop sparking after the flame starts. Dometic part number is 293 11 32-01/9. When control board replacement is necessary, I use the Dinosaur Electronics micro P-711.

Water Heaters

Two manufacturers make water heaters for RV's, Atwood and Suburban. Both provide 6 and 10 gallon sizes. Some are both gas and electric powered, and some are gas only. Atwood water heaters have an aluminum tank. Suburbans have a porcelain steel tank. Both types need to be flushed out annually.

This is a messy job so wear old clothes. First, turn off the water heater. Then turn off your water pump and shut off the city water supply. Then open the hot and cold kitchen sink faucets to relieve pressure from the system. Next open the water heater drain port from outside by removing the plug located on the center of the bottom of the tank. See picture (of an Atwood) below.

Use a ½ inch drive socket with extension. The Atwood has a plastic plug. The Suburban has a larger metal plug which has an aluminum anode rod attached. This rod is about 10 inches long and extends inside the tank. Let the water drain; stick your finger in the hole to stir up corrosion material. After the water drains, shut off the kitchen faucets and turn the water supply back on.

Hold your thumb on the drain hole for a few seconds to allow pressure to build inside the tank. Remove your thumb, allowing water and debris to blast out of the hole. Repeat until most debris is gone. Turn off the water supply.

If the Suburban anode rod has corroded away into a thin wire, replace the anode rod. Do not use anode rods in Atwood water heaters. Use the plastic plug only. Even though you can buy aftermarket magnesium rods for the Atwoods, you will ruin the aluminum pipe threads on the tank drain hole with the brass threads of the aftermarket rod through electrolysis. This ruins the tank. The iron Suburban tank needs the aluminum rod. If you fail to replace it you will rust out the bottom of the tank. Coat your plug or rod threads with pipe dope and replace the plug. Do not over tighten.

Open the hot water faucet and turn on the water supply, allowing the water heater tank to refill. When the water runs clear from the hot water faucet, you can turn the water heater back on.

If you attempt to heat water in a partially filled water heater, you will create super-heated steam in the air space above the water in the tank. This will cause the temperature/pressure relief valve to open, and you will get water seepage out of the valve. While this is harmless to do, it should not be done repeatedly. Older relief valves sometimes do not fully reclose. They will continuously seep and need to be replaced. It is best to always fully refill the tank before heating the water.

Another part of the regular water heater check is to clean the burner tube. Small spiders love to build nests inside this tube.

The first thing you will notice is the flame is orange and carbon is building up on the exhaust port. Water heaters should have a mild roar to the flame with a properly adjusted clean burner.

Remove the burner from the water heater. Use a small bottle brush to clean the inside of the tube. Look very carefully inside for debris. It only takes a small nest to disrupt the air flow. Replace and adjust the air screen (if equipped) for a blue flame.

Replacement of the pressure relief valve is tricky. It is difficult to get a pipe wrench onto it because of proximity to the top of the heater shroud. It is easiest to remove the exhaust vent assembly first. Then use a pipe wrench or large adjustable wrench to get it loose. Sometimes I stick a ½ inch drive extension into the hole for a wrench. The old valve is usually bent up pretty bad after removal, so always have the new valve on hand before you start. These valves are commonly available at most hardware stores. You do not need a factory replacement part. Some relief valves are ¾ and some are ½ inch pipe threads so check yours before going to the store.

Furnaces

The most common furnace is the Atwood "hydro flame" series. They are for the most part very trouble free. They do use a lot of propane. If used more than occasionally (are you a full timer?) you may need to replace the burner every few years.

Verify proper operation as follows. Make sure the thermostat is turned on. Advance the temperature to maximum. In older models, it will be up to 15 seconds before the fan starts. In newer models, the fan will start immediately. As soon as the fan starts an internal switch called a 'sail' switch closes. This signals the igniter circuit board to open the electrically controlled gas valve and to begin sparking to ignite the flame. The circuit board can detect the presence of flame through the high voltage igniter wire. The board measures the resistance to ground from the igniter probe, which is always surrounded by flame if the flame is on. When the probe is inside a flame front the resistance to ground is lower than when no flame is present. The control board can detect this subtle difference.

Heat flows from the furnace until the thermostat is satisfied. As soon as the set point is reached, the flame is extinguished. The fan will continue to run for 20 to 30 seconds after the flame stops.

If the control board fails to detect a flame, it will retry 3 times. You will not hear this going on because the fan will be on throughout the retries and mask the sound. If the retries fail, the control board will shut down the furnace and normally reset itself for three more tries the next time you call for heat from the thermostat.

The two parts that typically fail on furnaces are the control board and the burner. Rarely a fan motor will expire, but this has to be a very high mileage unit.

The control boards come in two varieties. Regular and "fan plus." If your unit continues to blow air for 15 seconds after the flame shuts down (thermostat satisfied), you have a "fan plus" unit. If your fan stops along with the flame (thermostat satisfied) you have an older standard unit.

Dinosaur Electronics makes 'better than factory' replacement control boards for furnaces. The most common is the UIB S fan plus. They have a lifetime warranty, are less expensive than OEM boards, and are almost exclusively used by repair shops. The control board is the most frequent part to fail on a furnace.

The second part that gives out is the burner. Over time the entire burner surface will overheat and rust out, resulting in an uneven flame front. It is sometimes difficult to diagnose if the burner is defective, or the control board is defective. The burner is much more difficult to remove. The gas must be shut off and disconnected. Some installations require removing the furnace from the rig to access the gas line connection to the gas valve. In other rigs the gas valve burner assembly can be extracted out the side of the rig without removing the furnace. If your furnace has an exterior hinged cover plate, you have a good chance that you can remove the burner assembly without removing the furnace. If yours has only an exhaust gas vent, you will have to remove the furnace for service.

Burners are inexpensive but parts numbers vary by model number. Control boards are over $100 but generally very easy to swap since they are usually secured only by a wing-nut and use plug-in connectors.

Make sure you use a piece of ¼ inch square hardware cloth or a mud dauber screen such as the Camco FUR series to prevent wasps from building nests inside your furnace. It is very difficult to clean out the interior of an infested furnace.

Chapter 8

Towing Vehicle Update

Water Pumps

Throughout my bombed Dodge towing career I have had trouble with engine heat. Whenever it was above 90°F outside I started to worry about my coolant temperature exceeding 220°F when on an extended uphill grade towing 15,000 pounds at full power. In California, we seldom have opportunity for this combination of events. Most grades are either too short to raise the engine temperature or the weather is too cool to create a problem.

At full power, my 5.9 liter Cummins runs at 32 psi of boost and has a sustained EGT of 1150°F. This power level (about 310 HP at the rear wheels) is perfectly safe for the engine as long as we can dissipate the heat from the cooling system.

I have been aware of this problem for years and had already substituted a Griffin triple core radiator (1 extra gallon of coolant capacity), replaced the viscous fan clutch, and replaced the thermostat.

A few years ago Cummins began offering the 6.7 liter diesel for Dodge trucks. This was to provide increased horsepower and to meet more stringent emissions requirements. The 6.7 Cummins produced about the same horsepower as my bombed 5.9 did.

An examination of the engine design showed that the 6.7 liter engine used essentially the same engine block as my 5.9, the main difference being 'sistered' cylinders as opposed to individual cylinders being cast into the head. Making two cylinders part of one casting made the cylinders stronger, which was needed because of the larger bore size.

I had heard that early 6.7 Cummins engines had a run of bad water pumps installed and found that people were substituting the water pump from the 5.9 Cummins because replacement pumps for the 6.7 were in short supply. One person went so far as to ask a

Cummins engineer if this substitution was safe. The engineer said it would work as long as the engine was not used to tow heavy loads up steep grades in hot weather. He said the older pump did not have sufficient flow to remove the heat.

Eureka! I called Gino's Garage and asked them to pull a new Gates pump off the shelf for both the 5.9 and the 6.7. Upon examination, the only difference was that the 6.7 pump had seven impeller blades and the 5.9 pump had five. The drive pulley, impeller penetration, 'o' ring, and mounting holes were identical! It seemed the water pump part of the 6.7 block casting had not been changed from the 5.9!

I installed a Cardone 5531412 pump (similar to the pump on the right pictured below) in my 5.9. It fit perfectly. It is also a very easy 30 minute job.

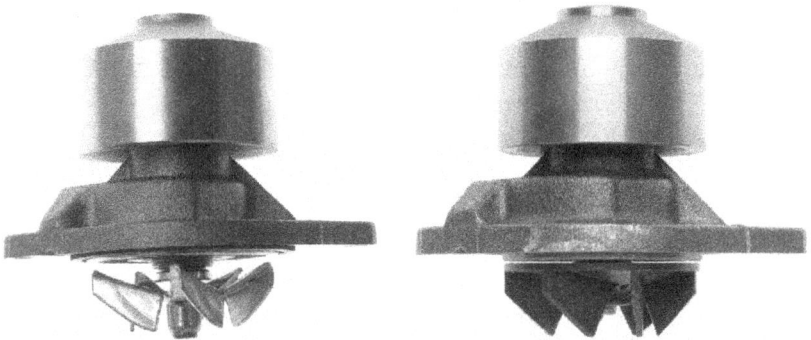

I purchased the more expensive Cardone pump because the impeller was cast iron and not plastic like the Gates pump. Cardone also claims to use higher quality bearings. The Cardone cast iron housing is slightly larger in the shaft area, which would contain these bearings.

The results are great. The truck runs 10°F cooler at all times, about 180° instead of 190° (I have a stock Cummins 190° high flow thermostat.) The coolant temperature never exceeds 190° even on the most severe grades. When it is a cold 33°F outside, the thermostat does its job but it takes the truck five to ten minutes to warm up sufficiently to run the heater. Since I have an exhaust brake and block heater, this seems no different than with the low flow stock pump.

EMI Revisited

Radio frequency noise in my mobile ham radio equipment is a constant problem. Noise from the alternator in Dodge pickups is a notorious offender. Alternator EMI infects the Dodge data bus and causes erratic operation of the PCM. Since the PCM controls the operation of the automatic transmission, the user experiences strange shift and lockup patterns when driving. This noise also raises the background noise level in the radio.

The best (and well documented) solution is to shield the alternator positive wire from the alternator to the alternator fuse on the PDC (fuse panel.) The best way to do this is to obtain a six foot piece of RG8X coaxial cable (available at West Marine and elsewhere.) Carefully cut the plastic jacket off of the cable using a razor knife, cutting a line along the length of the cable and peeling off the insulation. Don't cut too deeply; you don't want to cut the shield wires beneath. Next, just bunch up the shield braid and remove it from the center conductor.

After disconnecting the battery negative cables on the truck, remove the protective plastic cover and the black tape from the alternator wire. Disconnect the wire from the alternator and slide a four foot piece of the braid over the full length of the wire. Smooth out the braid. Solder a 6 inch #20 insulated wire pigtail onto the alternator end of the braid. Retape the wire, braid and all, being careful to not allow the braid to touch the alternator wire end terminals. Keep the braid at least 1 inch away from the terminals. Replace the cover and dress.

Using a two foot piece of braid, solder ring wire terminals onto each end. Solder the loose end of the #20 pigtail onto one end. Securely fasten that end to any available grounded screw on the alternator frame. Secure the other end to the body grounding screw, near the right battery box. You can find this screw by tracing the smaller wire from the right battery negative connector. Reconnect the batteries.

Another source of serious 7 MHz broadband noise came from the fan motor of my Derale transmission cooler. This problem was very tricky to find, since the transmission cooler fan only operated when fluid temperatures exceeded 180°F. The solution was a common mode choke with a .01uf capacitor on the input lead. Any common ferrite cores will do. Both the fan plus and minus leads are filtered.

Lift Pump Issues

Eventually everyone has diesel fuel lift pump issues on '99 through '03 Dodge diesels. I finally settled on 'gerotor' pump by Glacier Diesel. It was mounted and installed as per instructions. A similar pump is still available called a 'Raptor 100gph.'

As I was coming home down SR4 from Bear Valley, I noticed my fuel pressure 'idiot light' was blinking on occasionally. I made a mental note to change the 5 p.s.i. oil pressure sensor I was using to run the light when I got home. I had changed the sensor many times before because they began to give false readings after about a year's use. They were designed for oil and not diesel fuel, so they started leaking air after a while.

All of a sudden the truck stopped running. Engine dead. As I muscled the truck off the road (no power brakes, no power steering) I realized the idiot might be me.

I lifted the hood, and with the key on, measured the voltage to the lift pump relay. When you are using an after market lift pump, you must control it with a relay since the pump draws so much current. The voltage seemed low. I changed the relay. Voltage still low. I traced the wire back to its fuse, a 40 amp ATC fuse in a weatherproof fuse holder. The fuse was melted along with the fuse holder. I hastily twisted the wires together. Voltage normal.

Next I went through the drill to purge air from the injection pump. I was worried sick because I had recently installed an expensive top-of-the-line Blue Chip injection pump. Chip Fisher had said the pump could run without the lift pump, but for how long? The diesel sputtered to life, with diesel fuel everywhere. As I tightened the injectors and cleaned up the mess I gave thanks my injection pump was okay...

Chip Fisher had told me his 5 p.s.i. sensor was American made and did not leak. I should have believed him and trusted the light. My idiot light is a small LED in the dash, seen above the gear shift, below.

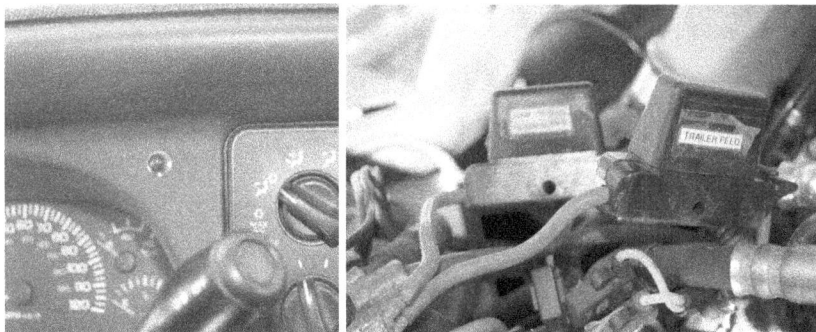

I replaced every fuse holder that contained a 40 amp ATC fuse with a 'MAXI' HHX fuse folder and the corresponding 40 amp 'MAXI' fuse. The problem had been that the current through the fuse was sufficient to cause the small blade contacts to overheat and melt. Never use 40 amp ATC fuses. If you really need 40 amp capacity, use a larger fuse holder. Note the fuse holders in the picture. Smaller low current ATC fuse holders are in the lower part of the picture for comparison. 'MAXI' fuse holders are available from most auto parts suppliers, RV dealers, and from West Marine Products.

Mini Inverter

It seems the kids now need to have 120VAC available in the truck cab to run their various electronic devices. It is also a necessity for me to be able to run power tools and my soldering gun when I am out on a service call. My truck has two batteries, so why not install a small modified sine wave inverter under the hood?

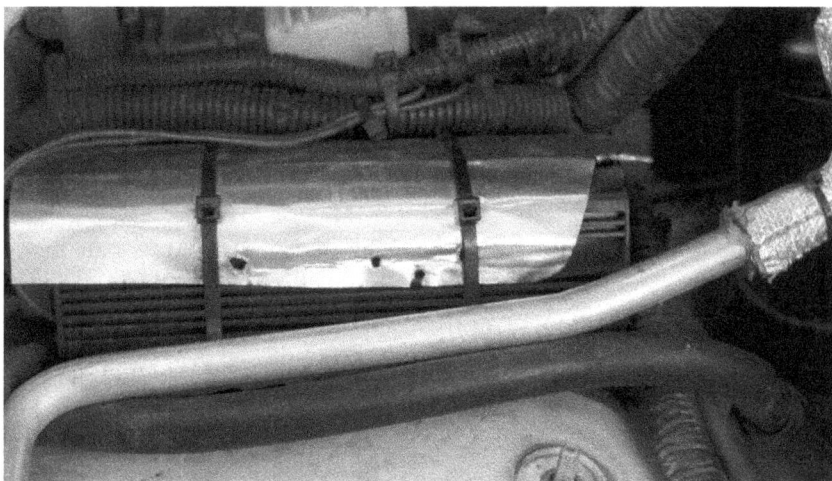

I used an inexpensive 800-watt unit available at most auto parts stores similar to a Samlex SAM-800-12. The inverter is tie wrapped into place in the space between the PCM and the air cleaner. It has a piece of aluminum flashing fashioned into a cover to keep water splashes off. I use #4 cables for the short 2-foot run to the right battery. I opened up the inverter and soldered a wire pair (#22 speaker wire) across the on-off switch. The wire is routed across and through the firewall opening to a toggle switch mounted near the driver.

A six-foot computer power cord is plugged in to the inverter and routed under the passenger seat. The female end is cut off and routed through the floorboard into a convenience outlet mounted under the passenger seat. This provides more than sufficient power for the in cab needs, including an XBOX 360. Since it is a MSW inverter, some devices do not work properly. If you are really picky you could install a pure sine wave inverter, but they are slightly larger and more expensive.

Another nice accessory I use constantly are the pair of Contico L3725-4 Pro Tuff Boxes in the bed of the pickup. These boxes are flush with the bed rails and are lockable. Since they are flush, they can't readily be seen from outside the truck and they do not interfere with the 5th wheel. They are prevented from side to side movement by gas containers and a bed bar cross member. I use additional plastic gasoline containers as spacers between the back-to-back Tuff Boxes to allow them to both stand opened without hitting each other in the center of the bed.

The 5th wheel is plugged into a seven-way plug installed in the bed on the left side just forward of the fender housing. This is the best location for this plug since it can be easily reached with the 5th wheel connected. The wiring is just tagged onto the existing seven-way plug wiring on the drawbar.

I'm on my third rebuild of my Dana 70 differential. I believe that shoddy factory workmanship was the cause, since the pinion bearing seal was leaking from the factory and the local Dodge dealer never got it right. A reputable aftermarket repair shop did the latest rebuild. They cemented the carrier bearings onto the carrier so they cannot spin. I believe the gear oil got too hot while towing so now I use only Amsoil Severe Gear lubricant and monitor the temperature of the rear end from the cab. See picture below. I have had no more trouble; I pull over on those occasions where the fluid reaches 200°F. This only occurs pulling doubles (17,000 pounds) when the outside temperature is over 95°F and I am going up a grade.

You can also see the 2 low vacuum switch above the gauge, which allows the use of low range in the transfer case without four wheel drive. This comes in very handy for parking the rig on grades.

Dropping the Fiver

We had just left Sacramento on our way home after Christmas. I had noticed the hitch made a funny sound as I had hooked up to leave 20 minutes ago, but gave it no mind since I had checked the jaw and it was closed on the 5er draw pin. I was cruising west on I80, passing through Rio Linda. Then, WHAM! It sounded like a mega blowout! I looked in to mirror and the fifth wheel was resting on the pickup box side rails! I eased off the throttle and nudged off onto the shoulder.

The pin box was disconnected, just suspended in space behind the hitch, supported by the trailer cross member, which was resting on the box rails.

This was not the first time I had dropped it. Last time it was before leaving Plaskett Creek Campground. But then it was different. I was a novice with the fifth wheel and wasn't aware of the safety checks needed before hitting the road. So this time, I wasn't panicked, just angry, as I lowered the landing legs and raised the rig off of the truck. I pulled out the tool box and removed the hitch plate. Underneath I found that the retaining teeth had become unmeshed allowing the jaw to open. So I was the victim of shoddy workmanship.

All the major moving parts were held in place with compression washer-nuts similar to the failed one above. They were slipped onto pins, which served as hinge points as well as slide retainers. The critical washer holding the pin retainer gear had cracked and slipped down enough to allow the mechanism to disengage. A pretty sad statement about the workmanship on this '22.5'K hitch.

The pins were 5/16 inch in diameter and I had some stainless steel 5/16 flat washers. I removed the critical compression nuts and slid a flat washer onto the pins.

I turned on the inverter. I drilled 1/8 inch holes laterally through the pins, just flush with the top of the new washers. I then put cotter pins in the holes and reassembled the hitch plate. Next it was off to the nearest freeway exit and in to Home Depot. I bought more washers and stainless cotter pins. I pulled off the hitch plate and discarded all the remaining compression washers, replacing them with flat washers and cotter pins. All was well except for the $10,000 repair job, which included a new box for the pickup. And all because someone saved a few pennies using inferior parts and assembly techniques.

So now I completely disassemble my hitch plate annually for lubrication and inspection. The manufacturer's instructions call for periodic inspection, but they don't say what to look for. Now I know.

Chapter 9

Entertainment and Security

The Living Room

Having the same home theater on the road as you have at home seems to be the goal now. We are no longer satisfied with a small TV set and a car radio. Times have changed and customers are demanding more and more in their rigs. Fortunately, most of the necessary components are getting smaller in size without sacrificing much in quality.

My first rig had a 6 inch portable TV and a car radio that would also play cassette tapes and we though we were in heaven. The next rig had a built-in 19 inch 4:3 television along with a combo radio and DVD player. We also had built-in stereo speakers. The upgrade cycle had begun.

Even now I change devices as technology improves, so the current AV setup is always a work in progress. The latest version in the living room area is pictured below.

On the top shelf we find dual quad duplex outlets for plugging in all the various chargers for cell phones, cameras, camcorders and so on. Next is the line level 5.1 decoder. I use a HDV-18A Chinese unit from lunashops.com. The Mocha JY-M2 has the same specifications. These little boxes accept two optical inputs as well as two coaxial inputs. These four digital inputs and the output channel volume levels are changed with its remote control. It runs on 12 volts DC and all 6 outputs are RCA jacks on the rear panel. I use this device so that I can use the Sony MHC series mini component hi-fi (pictured on the lowest shelf) as the left and right front speakers in the 5.1 system. The subwoofer (not pictured) is in the cabinet below the Sony unit, and accepts subwoofer input from the Sony as well as from the 5.1 unit.

Also in the subwoofer space is an AudioSource Amp 50 stereo amplifier, which powers the left and right rear surround speakers. These small 3 way speakers are wall mounted in the rear of the living space. I use a scavenged Labtec PC speaker system for the center channel; the PC system is stuffed behind the components on the top shelf. It also runs on 12 volts and the left and right channels are both fed with the 5.1 center channel output of the HDV-18A.

Optical digital outputs from the Mitsubishi Unisen LT40164 40 inch TV, the Directv HDDVR, as well as coaxial digital outputs from the LG BD550 Blu Ray player and the old Panasonic PV-D744S VCR/DVD player are connected to the 5.1 decoder digital inputs. As you can see, when you change the TV video input source, you must also change to the corresponding digital audio source when using 5.1. Naturally, the TV can be used without the 5.1 system e.g. if you want to use the Sony system to play music (inside or outside) while using headphones or TV speakers to watch TV.

Next on the top shelf is the DirecTv HDDVR. Its HDMI output is fed to outdoor TV's and its component HD signal output is connected to the TV. Its video output is sent to a small modulator box, which converts the signal to an NTSC TV signal on analog channel 3. This output is fed to the standard Winegard RV antenna switch (located on top of the DVR) for satellite viewing via legacy 4:3 TV sets.

On the middle shelf left corner we find an almost invisible video to HDMI converter for up scaling video devices such as the camcorder and VCR for input to the digital TV. The device to be up-converted is selected by the a/video/svideo switch pictured on the right of the middle shelf. Since the a/v switch also switches the audio input to the Sony system, it can select an ipod jack as well for playback of MP3 audio devices. The LG BluRay player sits on top of the legacy Panasonic player in the center of the middle shelf. The LG BluRay player analog output is fed to another channel 3 modulator, for display on legacy 4:3 TV's via the Winegard antenna switch.

The small black box to the left of the LG is a c.crane Justice AM Antenna controller. This antenna is used to pick up weak AM radio stations that otherwise could not be received. This amplified antenna is connected to the Sony system AM antenna jack.

Above the a/video switch is a box that switches the svideo output from the a/v switch to either an external svideo feed (for outside projection) or to the up-converter (for viewing on the TV.) On the lower shelf left are the Sony system speaker switches, which allow the Sony music/5.1 system to be heard in the forward bedroom or outside.

This configuration is quite complex but allows full flexibility in playback with any source media. It also is compact and has no redundancy. Velcro is used to prevent component shift.

All components in the entertainment center are protected by small single circuit surge protectors from Walmart. These were installed after the extensive repairs made in Texas as a result of the melted neutral incident.

Infrared repeater senders can be seen in front of the DVR, the BluRay player, and the Sony component system. This allows these devices to be controlled from outside the rig, using any of the infrared remote controls. The receiving 'eye for these repeater/senders is mounted high in the living room window overlooking the outside entertainment area. This makes it very easy to control the music volume or to switch DVR/music/TV channels from outside.

Outside TV's can be placed near the rear slide out as well as in the basement sliding multipurpose frame, each with its own HD programming. Cabling allows placement as far as fifty feet away from the rig.

The Bedroom

The entertainment system in the bedroom is much simpler.

The entire setup is in the space between the cabinet and the ceiling. On the right is the second DirecTv HDDVR It is set up for RF remote control so the remote control does not have to be within eye shot of the DVR. This allows DVR control from outside the rig. The HDMI output feeds a two way Rocketfish HDMI splitter (almost invisible on the left end.) Its two outputs are connected to two fifty foot HDMI cables; one is routed to the living room TV and the other is coiled in the basement for the outside TV. The DVR component feed plus L/R audio is connected to the bedroom TV.

Above the DVR is a small Sony DVD player, which is connected via HDMI to the TV. In the middle of the picture is another LG BluRay player. Its HDMI output is also cabled to the basement for remote use by the outside TV. Its component HD output is connected to the small shiny box next to it. This box converts the component HD signal to a 720p HDMI signal for use by the bedroom TV.

The #3 TV feed (from the Winegard antenna switch in the living room) also connects to the bedroom TV, allowing viewing of park cable or off-air HDTV. This feed runs through a TV splitter behind the TV, which also allows the basement outside TV to view off-air TV in addition to HD BluRay and DVR content fed from the bedroom devices.

Above is a picture of the pencil drawing I keep on hand in my rig to show the detail of the AV wiring. Whenever changes are made to the system, this drawing is updated.

Compartment Locks

Every RV ever shipped seems to come with the same compartment keys. Dealers keep them stocked. They are as common as bread in a grocery store. They all have CH751 stamped on them. If you have these keys for your outside compartments, you have no lock security at all!

At the very least switch to RV Designer L54x version hardware, as pictured below. The L325 series are even better with Ace style tumblers. Or substitute any high quality 5/8 cylinder length tubular cam lock. Depending on the door thickness, you may need 5/8, 7/8, or 1 1/8 length cylinders, or no lock at all! It seems kind of stupid to lock a compartment that does nothing but store a shore power cord. Why have to carry a key to unlock something that contains nothing of value?

The Pantry

My pantry cabinet used to fly open on the road, emptying its contents onto the kitchen floor. A big mess. And cans can dent things as they roll around going down the highway. Time for a fix. I added a keyed drawer lock to the pantry. These locks are commonly available at hardware stores, similar to National Mfg. N183772 available on Amazon. The base is spaced away from the door with washers to make the bolt strike the center of the wooden door frame. Use a little chalk on the bolt to mark the drilling location on the door frame. Then carefully drill a series of small 1/8 inch holes into the door frame. Use a small wood chisel to clean up the holes into a slot that will accept the bolt.

This lock also works well to keep children out of the pantry! You can also work this trick on sliding drawers or any cabinet you want to lock. I have modified a drawer in the bedroom to hold small arms. I used a drawer lock and installed a plywood partition in the drawer cabinet space to prevent access via adjacent drawers.

Another drawer lock was used on an overhead cabinet in the living room. This time, security was only a secondary issue. The cabinet contains a Kenwood TS-440 ham radio and I did not want it to fall out while on the road.

Another neat security trick is to buy a group of similarly keyed long shank padlocks. These are used to lock bicycles, motorcycles, gas cans, fifth wheel hitch release levers, and most anything you can get a cable around. You need these most in urban camping environments, but they also give you a nice feeling when you leave your dry camp site to go to the grocery store.

Safes

An essential accessory that very few rigs have is a safe! It doesn't have to be big, just very difficult to break in to. Small drop boxes or floor safes can be mounted with blind screws under stairwells. We use our safe for passports, car titles, cash, and jewelry while traveling.

The small floor safe above (a Monarch Value Vault) is screwed into the left adjacent stair riser. The screws are invisible from outside the safe. The space under the stairway is inaccessible. Small safes such as this one can be bought for under $75.

Time to go RVing....

Notes

Suppliers and Vendors

Alfa Network Inc.
http://www.alfa.com.tw/product_category.php?pc=3
American RV Company
https://www.americanrvcompany.com/
Astron Corporation
http://www.astroncorp.com/
Atwood
http://www.atwoodmobile.com/
AudioSource
http://www.audiosource.net/products/electronics/amplifiers/amp-50/overview/
Blue Chip Diesel
http://www.bluechipdiesel.com/
Camco
http://www.camco.net/Products/?d=RV
Cardone Industries Inc.
http://www.cardone.com/
C.Crane
http://www.ccrane.com/antennas/am-antennas/twin-coil-ferrite-am-antenna.aspx#.UQ3flKzhcls
Continental Commercial Products (Contico)
http://www.continentalcommercialproducts.com/retail.html
Derale Performance
http://www.derale.com/
Digi-Key Corporation
www.digikey.com
Dinosaur Electronics
http://www.dinosaurelectronics.com/
Dometic
http://www.dometic.com/enus/Americas/USA/RV-Products/
DonRowe.com
http://www.donrowe.com/index.html
DTT Transmission
http://www.dieseltrans.com/
Geno's Garage
http://www.genosgarage.com/
Goerend Transmission Inc.
http://www.goerend.com/
Home Depot
http://www.homedepot.com/buy/estate-design-arlington-24-in-panoramic-wall-mounted-electric-fireplace-in-black-wmar.html#.UQgq9azhcls

Notes

Suppliers and Vendors, continued

LunaShops (China)
http://www.lunashops.com/goods.php?id=294
Magnetek Parallax Power
http://www.parallaxpower.com/
Monarch Coin and Security
http://www.monarchcoin.com/other-security-products
Norcold/Thetford
http://www.thetford.com/
NuWa Industries
http://www.nuwa.com/
Phoenix Faucets
http://www.faucets.com/store/category/faucets/recreational
Progressive Dynamics Inc.
https://www.progressivedyn.com/rv_products.html
Radio Shack Nibbler
http://www.radioshack.com/product/index.jsp?productId=2289712
RV Designer
http://www.rvdesigner.com/prodview.asp?ci=11&pi=168
Samlex
http://www.samlexamerica.com/
SeeLeveL Gauges
http://www.rvgauge.com/rv.htm
Suburban Airxcel
http://www.rvcomfort.com/suburban/
Suncor Stainless
http://www.suncorstainless.com/railing-bimini
Surge Guard RV Power Protection
http://www.surgeguard.com/34750_LCD.html
TE Connectivity Corcom
http://www.cor.com/Series/RFI.asp
Weber Grills
http://www.weber.com/explore/grills/gas-portable
West Marine Products
http://www.westmarine.com/
Winegard
http://www.winegard.com/mobile/index.php
Wise Sales BERGS
http://www.wisesales.com/bergs-dual-feed-extended-run-tank-for-honda.html#.UQgvO6zhclt
Xantrex
http://www.xantrex.com/

www.ingramcontent.com/pod-product-compliance
Lightning Source LLC
Chambersburg PA
CBHW021343090426
42742CB00008B/726